A SAUCERFUL OF TEA

Brian Southall

pop publishing

A SAUCERFUL OF TEA
Brian Southall

First published 2022 by Poppublishing
Text © Brian Southall 2022
This work © Poppublishing
Paperback: ISBN: 9798420745229
Also published as an Amazon Kindle ebook

For further information about this book please contact
poppublishing@gmail.com

The author's thanks go to David Roberts at poppublishing
for all his support, help and advice and to Sophie Putland
for Michael's photographs and also to Chelmsford's top
'mod' Liz Woodcraft for her much appreciated pearls
of wisdom.

For Pat - the Julie to my Terry
in a Waterloo Sunset

Front cover photo:
Could the front cover be a photo of rock 'n' roll hero Billy
Fury relaxing in his garden?
The trousers are tight, the shoes are sharp and the quiff is
greased in place as author Brian Southall does his best to
look the part as a smiling teenage idol

"I'm fed up being a cub reporter.
They never make news,
just sit in a circle going dib dib dib all the time."

Kenneth Williams
Round The Horne, BBC May 1968

Chapter 1

SOME OF THE JUICY BITS

I knew I'd cracked it within ten minutes of arriving for my first real job interview. I was going to be a journalist, a scribe, a wordsmith.

The job was as a junior reporter on the *Essex Chronicle* newspaper based in Chelmsford, years before the major town established as a Roman settlement in AD60 and named Caesaromagus, ever dreamt of becoming a city. This was despite the fact that the local football team was called Chelmsford City and there was a cathedral which, we were all told at school, were all you needed to be called a city. But, apparently, that was all a lie.

To be honest back then in the early sixties I knew very little about Chelmsford despite arriving, aged six, in 1954 from Worcestershire. I had heard of Marconi, the inventor of wireless who opened his factory in the town in 1899 (which I didn't know) because he was famous and it was one of the four 'houses' we had at the grammar school I attended. The other houses were also named after prominent local companies: Crompton (who had made electrical systems and lamps from 1878); Hoffman (manufacturers of ball bearings since 1898) and a local builder called French who began building things in 1895.

The town's population was around 55,000 (it grew to 58,000 by 1971) and among the most prominent home-grown celebrities were (and again I didn't know) Sir Walter Mildmay who was appointed Chancellor of the Exchequer by Queen Elizabeth 1 in 1566, anti-slavery campaigner and social reformer Anne Knight, born in 1786, plus, and this was more up my alley, the actress Carole Lesley who was born Maureen Rippingale in 1935 and who I had seen in the 1960 film *Doctor In Love* but not in her less famous fol-low-up *What a Whopper* with Adam Faith.

And while Mildmay bought the manor of Moulsham in Chelmsford and had Mildmay Road named after him and Knight had Anne Knight House, a Grade II listed building named in her honour (although it is now a bar and restaur-ant), Lesley is remembered by a block of flats called Lesley Court, built on the site of the local Pavilion cinema where she had worked as an usherette.

In addition to these historical landmarks, Chelmsford also boasted a selection of estates, built to deal with the post-World War II population explosion and the town's growth in the 1960s as part of the ever-increasing commuter belt around London. While Westlands, Springfield Park and Chignal were predominantly council-owned properties, Moulsham Lodge and a second Springfield estate were both slightly more up-market collections of private homes.

At the other end of the market were the combined efforts of Boarded Barns and Rainsford (both built in the 1920s) that sort of melded into Melbourne which was first de-veloped in the 1930s and completed in the 1960s with the creation of the town's tallest building – a council owned 14-storey tower block of flats built in 1962. Back then this

area was considered by many (certainly the local constabulary) to be the 'arse-end' of Chelmsford and was home to
many a local villain and thug.

However, inspired by my journalist father, and further
convinced by a poor academic performance, which included failing all seven GCSE exams, I decided that writing
for a newspaper was what I wanted to do and Chelmsford
was the town I was eager to cover, investigate and if necessary, expose to thousands of readers. Those GCSE failures?
For the record they were English Literature and Language,
History, Geography, Religious Education, Physics and Technical Drawing, while I was barred from taking Maths and
French after getting single figure marks in the so-called
'mock' exams.

Before my career as a journalist could begin, there was
the not so small matter of an interview to get through although in the end it turned out to be something of a doddle.

The interrogations were held on a Saturday morning in
the canteen of the *Chronicle's* brand new offices on a road
called Westway which were just across the road from
Britvic and Marconi Marine, the only two companies where
I had ever been gainfully employed since leaving school.
And, as all three were just a five minute walk from where
I lived with my parents in Widford Grove, I never had an
excuse for being late for anything.

The house we lived in - me, my brother and parents –
was a sort of freebie as my dad got it as part of his job as
sports editor of the *Essex Weekly News*. I didn't know the
ins and outs of the deal, although I assumed he must have
paid rent, just that it was a comfortable three bedroomed
semi-detached house with, in estate agents' parlance, "sep
wc, det grge, attctve grdn." The going price for one back in
the mid-fifties was around £2000 and had risen to nearly

£4000 by 1964 but as my father was never going to buy it, it was all academic.

At Britvic, the world famous drinks company that made fruit juices and Babycham, which was the first remotely alcoholic drink that most teenage girls tried in the sixties, I was a teenage virgin thrown into a lioness's den of older women. How old they were I didn't actually know or care, they were just a terrifyingly smutty bunch of ladies who were years ahead of their time when it came to sexual harassment.

Most of us youngsters working there had taken jobs as temporary summer holiday employment and we were assigned to a rota of mundane tasks, each lasting half an hour, following the progress of bottles from empty to full along a constantly moving belt. We began by putting empty bottles on the track then moved on to look at them through a magnifying glass to check for chips before watching them fill with juice, ensuring the bottle tops were on properly and then putting the filled bottles into crates. Finally we had to move the filled crates and put them somewhere to be collected by delivery men – there were no such things as delivery women!

All these jobs were carried out alongside the not so enticing sirens of the bottling room whose non-stop banter about cute bums, tight trousers and our youthful inexperience made us blush with embarrassment and made the whole tedious, brain-numbing experience even worse.

For no good reason I got a sort of promotion away from the bottling room into the juice room where we pierced holes in large cans of fruit juice with huge metal spikes and then poured the undiluted liquid into vast vats, where it was processed into the tasty, sugar-stuffed nectar of the gods that went on sale to the public as fruit juice..

Unlike the bottle belt, it was a job with regular, irregular breaks as once all the vats were filled we could relax until the next round. This involved some lads (and lasses, as we were overseen by what became known as the juicy fruit ladies) having a fag break, some sunbathing if it was warm enough or, as the factory backed onto Chelmsford's main Crematorium, amusing ourselves by watching the pall of smoke rise from the chimneys and, if anybody had thought to bring in the local paper, we might even check the death notices to see who was literally going up in flames.

Britvic operated a strict no nicking stuff policy so one of the challenges we faced was to get past the guardhouse with a few bottles of fruit juice or even Babycham (one of my mum's favourite tipples) without getting caught and fired. You might go for a bottle or two down the trousers or in your pocket if you wanted to impersonate Elvis in his early sexiest period when he used a soda bottle to create a similar look but for an entirely different reason.

However putting bottles in a holdall or lunch bag, wrapped in something soft to stop them clinking, was another way to get out with your booty and this was my preferred method of skulduggery. Not many of us were caught as I don't think the security men were that bothered about the odd bottle going AWOL, but you had to avoid becoming a regular suspect.

When all the fun at the factory came to an end it was time for me go and find a proper job and in those days, even with the few measly qualifications I had managed to scrape together at a second GCSE sitting, there was still a choice of employment albeit not at the high end of the job market. I knew exactly what I wanted to do but this wasn't the right time so I took a job as a clerk – and all you needed back then to become a clerk was the ability to stand upright and

write your own name - with the large international radar
company that was around the corner from my home.

My education was at the esteemed Chelmsford Technical
High School, one of three grammar schools in the town
along with King Edward VI for boys and Chelmsford High
School for girls. These stood alongside secondary modern,
or 'sec mod' schools as we called them, which were considered – mainly by parents as us kids couldn't really care
less – a level below the education offered to us know-alls
who had passed the 11+ examination.

Among them were Moulsham, Rainsford, Sandon,
Broomfield, Boswells (in Springfield), Westlands and the
Roman Catholic Blessed John Payne school and the difference was highlighted when it came to sports as us grammar
school kids didn't deign to mix it with these second division secondary outfits. We fought it out against our equals
from grammar schools in Braintree, Maldon, Newport (not
Wales) and even Colchester but in all my time at the Tech
(where I was 'capped' in football, cricket, rugby and athletics) we never took on our near neighbours from King Edward VI school for reasons I never knew.

However, if like me at eleven, you were on the cusp –
possibly smart enough for a grammar school education but
more academically inclined towards a secondary school –
you had a chance to talk your way into higher education
through something called an oral exam. This, as it turned
out, involved meeting with the headmaster/mistress and
deputy head to answer questions, read a bit and solve a
couple of puzzles.

I qualified for one of these at the Technical High School's
original building in Victoria Road, before it moved to
Patching Hall Lane in the late 1950s. I met with the head
Dr Stevens and his right hand man for my oral and while I

don't recall much about the exam I do know that it didn't involve any written work (the clue was in the name I suppose).

I was asked to read from *Moby Dick* by Herman Melville which was one of only two films that my father had ever taken me to see (*Battle of The River Plate* was the other). I remember that when it got to a bit about the 'blasted whale' I hummed and hesitated as I knew the word 'blasted' was a swear word. Undaunted, with my future education in my own hands, I ploughed on and also managed to explain the quickest way across a matchbox from two not quite opposite corners.

However the whole thing very nearly fell apart when I was asked what career I wanted to pursue. I was eleven with no thoughts back then towards journalism so plucked out of the air something which sounded suitably grandiose. "I'd like to be a civil engineer," I blurted for no good reason other than to impress. But then came the million dollar question I hadn't anticipated. "Interesting. And what do you think they do?" All I could say in reply was "I don't know but they are really nice to people."

For some reason – whether it was down to my natural charm, boyish innocence or rapier wit (all mixed in with some Worcestershire sauce) – a few weeks later I surprisingly found myself invited to join the boys and girls (it was a mixed grammar) in the premier league at the Tech High with its smart blue blazer, red and blue striped tie and quartered cap – the girls had berets or straw hats which looking back seems a bit sexist.

Six months after leaving my five years at the Tech - and with my Britvic experience to fall back on as time spent in the workplace with grown-up people - I began work as a clerk for Marconi Marine. They were based in a large flat-roofed and uninspiring concrete edifice called Elettra House which some historians claim was named after founding father Guglielmo Marconi's yacht although he had a daughter, born in 1930, whose middle name was also Elettra.

During the Second World War the yacht was commandeered by the German Navy and turned into a warship which was sunk by the RAF in 1944, when his daughter was 14 years of age. As the building which was now my professional workplace was opened in the early 1960s it's a toss-up whether the powers-that-be named it after a sunken Nazi warship or a beloved daughter.

Marconi Marine, and the name was a bit of a giveaway, were involved with things that happened at sea although for the life of me I never really mastered what it was all about. There were lots of bits of paper with the names of ships on them and I think the company had something to do with their radar equipment but even after twenty-odd weeks behind a desk in a huge anonymous brown and grey office that reminded me of the one Tony Hancock railed against in his film *The Rebel*, I still had no real idea what they did or, and more to the point, what I was supposed to be doing. My leaving present to the company was a drawer full of unprocessed forms which I now rather hope didn't put anyone in peril on the sea.

But now was the time – late 1964 - when things started to move in the direction I wanted. Encouraged by my father, who perhaps hoped I might follow in his journalistic footsteps as my older brother was inclined towards more practical (and useful) things like engines, machines and mechanics, I had applied for the job at the *Essex Chronicle*, been invited to an interview and duly arrived, in my Sunday best even though it was a Saturday, at just after 9am, prepared to sit and wait my turn as editor Ken Andrews and assistant editor Josie Spargo interrogated the anxious aspirants.

Surprisingly the fact that my dad was sports editor on the rival local paper and I went to school with the son of my prospective new editor somehow weighed in my favour when Andrews walked into the canteen. He was a bear of a man with the bow-legged walk of a cowboy and when he came face to face with the more than a dozen nervous hopefuls it all seemed very daunting but within minutes both my heart and the weight on my shoulders were suddenly lifted.

"We'll meet with each of you this morning and then make a decision over the next week or so," explained Andrews. "So please be patient, help yourself to a cup of something and maybe take a look at a copy of the paper."

He then looked around the room in search of something or somebody, saw me and simply said, "Hi Brian. Why don't you go away for an hour or so and come back later when we'll have a chat." That was it, the time when I knew I was destined to be junior reporter and follow in the footsteps of my father - unless I got run over by a bus while I was away.

It wasn't subtle and it was certainly desperately unfair on my fellow applicants, most of whom were definitely older, probably better educated and perhaps even more qualified than me. I can only assume that they quickly worked out that the wheels had just come off their carefully planned journey into journalism, but I didn't care as I was on the verge of a new career.

A few hours later Ken Andrews, who had a five o'clock shadow at all times of the day, explained that he knew I had been writing sports reports for my father since I was 15 and, courtesy of his son, that I did well in English at school where every other subject was either simply boring or more boring. And despite me having only two GCSE 'O' levels (you were supposed to have three to become a journalist and I only had obtained English Literature and Geography at the second attempt), he also worked out that at just 17 years of age I would be dead keen, very impressionable and, perhaps most importantly, dirt cheap.

And cheap I was. I think my weekly wage as a 17 year old cub reporter was somewhere between £7 and £8 while the average weekly wage was, apparently, about 17 quid although a postman aged between 18 and 45 would only pocket around £12. 10s. 6d. ((£12.53p) a week which was still more than me.

Back at the *Chronicle*, in return for my pittance of a wage, I was duly indentured to the paper which meant I couldn't leave for three years and, in return, they tried their best to teach me all I needed to know to become a future Keith Waterhouse, James Cameron or Hugh McIlvenny. This education involved me swanning along to Colchester's North East Essex Technical College in Sheepen Road each Friday to attend an NUJ course. The whole thing climaxed after three years with a Proficiency Test which I don't remember ever taking but, as I didn't get fired, I must have scraped through somehow.

Chapter 2

VISITING THE STREET OF SHAME

When I joined the *Chronicle* in 1964, it had been go-ing for exactly 200 years and was owned by the local Handley family with R.A.F. Handley in place as edit-or-in-chief. When it was launched in 1764 it was described as "not simply a newspaper but a repository for every kind of useful knowledge" and reading this made me wonder what I had let myself in for … was it a local paper or an encyclopaedia and what sort of knowledge was considered to be not useful?

I didn't meet the big boss until after I arrived in the edit-orial offices on the first floor of the Westway building and when we did meet, it very quickly became clear that he wasn't keen on me being there. Oddly in all my time at the paper I never did find out what the initials R.A.F. stood for as he always Mr Handley to me.

The often drink-sodden old boy with his trim moustache and powerful regimental stride – was he actually in the RAF we wondered - was worried both that I wasn't properly qualified and that my father was sports editor on the rival paper the *Essex Weekly News*. He warned me in no uncertain terms that he would be keeping an eye on me to make sure I didn't pass on to my dad any of the scoops I might search out and expose. It didn't occur to the old buffer that my dad was more likely to pass tips on to me – which he did on more than one occasion.

Anyway with Andrews at my back – and his son Rodney now on the paper as well (now that was nepotism) – I set out down a new path which would initially involve me in learning shorthand (Ng = ing, S = ess and Ch = chay), sitting through endless local council meetings, visiting fetes and carnivals and writing out wedding reports. But I was following in the footsteps of Charles Dickens, Ernest Hemingway and Dylan Thomas and who knew where they might lead.

My new profession was perhaps the natural path for me in light of my father's long journalistic career and my visits to the offices of the *Weekly News* in Chelmsford High Street (it's now a Scottish bank) which stretched back to my junior school days. Although I didn't show any signs of being interested in (or having any talent for) writing until I was in my early teens, I did spend a lot of time in the offices and works of the *Weekly News* and something must have sunk in.

It certainly wasn't the idea of a glamourous future informing the 'great unwashed' (a slightly unfair term used to describe the less well educated and less well off) and anybody else who was interested about the goings on around them. My father went to work on a bike, took sandwiches for lunch or had them delivered by his in-house delivery boy (me) and used the same bicycle or the local bus service to go to football and cricket matches whatever the weather.

My father (far right) was sports editor of the *Essex Weekly News* for over 30 years and always followed the careers of local footballers who 'made good'. This included having dinner with these four goalkeepers (l to r) Barry Daines (Tottenham Hotspur), Bryan King (Millwall & Coventry), Dave Danson (West Ham) and Mervyn Day (West Ham & Leeds), who all had connections with Chelmsford

When he eventually learnt to drive, somewhere in the early sixties, he plumped for a bright red Renault Dauphine which would have cost around £700 new – which ours wasn't. It was in this that we drove all the way through France to northern Spain (along with our near neighbours in their Ford Anglia) for a 10 day holiday somewhere near Sitges. The car was described at the time as "the prettiest little four seater in the world" but whoever wrote that had never had to sit in it for three days and even sleep in it (with three other people) in a forest just outside Paris. Pretty it may have been but comfortable and roomy it was not.

Eventually he traded up for a more glamourous gold Renault Gordino before settling on a mighty Rover 80 (or it might have been a Rover 90 – they all looked the same to me) in solid black. It seemed huge, had sumptuous leather seats and would have cost around £1200 new - again it wasn't.

When I was around 16 I got my first real glimpse of investigative journalism when my father arranged for me to go to the Fleet Street offices of, I think, the *Daily Mail* to scour through back issues of the paper in search of information. This involved me taking the train from Chelmsford to Liverpool Street via a cheap day return ticket which cost about 9s (45p) and then on to Holborn on the Central Line.

I can't remember exactly what I was supposed to be looking for but it involved the footballer Bobby Mason who had left First Division Wolverhampton Wanderers (where he was valued at around £20,000) and signed as a full time professional with non-league Chelmsford City.

At that time players registered with League clubs could move to a non-league club on what was called a 'free' transfer and Mason's 'free' move to Chelmsford prompted outrage within the 92 clubs in the Football League. It was legal but frowned on and it wasn't long before the authorities clamped down, stamped out all future moves of this sort and banned Chelmsford City from applying for Football League membership for five years.

If the football authorities were upset, it was nothing compared to the anger felt within the ranks of Chelmsford City who had invested heavily in an effort to gain election to the League but now found themselves barred.

The Clarets, as Chelmsford were called, had been established in 1878 and when it came to finding a club mascot somebody, for reasons best known to them, decided it should be something that rhymed with 'claret' ... which obviously meant it had to be a parrot! Now during my time visiting the club's New Writtle Street Ground, for nigh on 30 years from 1957, I never saw hide nor hair (or beak nor feather) of a parrot. And during their golden era in the 1960s, they won the Southern League in 1968, after finishing second in 1964, the team ran out to 'Waltzing Bugle Boy' by Frank Chacksfield's Orchestra. This was when the club was managed by ex-Coventry player and manager Bill Frith and benefitted from the exploits of local lad Tony Butcher who made a record 560 appearances and scored a record 286 goals for the City.

Incidentally it was the same Frith who scuppered my faint hopes of becoming a professional footballer – a dream every boy cherished back then and probably still today. I had represented Mid-Essex in an under 18s team but when my father persuaded Frith to come along and watch me, the old pro commented, "Tell him it doesn't hurt to kick the ball sometimes." Apparently he was less than impressed with my more destructive than constructive style of play while I took the view that I was ahead of my time as the likes of Nobby Stiles, Norman Hunter and Peter Storey (all described in the press as 'destroyers') went on to play for England.

The story involving Bobby Mason's transfer was what prompted my father to send me off to London to search through back issues of the Mail for some tit-bits of news or comment that would help the cause. My research involved me being put in a slightly claustrophobic room (which did actually overlook Fleet Street) where I trawled through heavyweight bound copies of the newspaper. Did I find anything? I don't remember but if I did it obviously didn't make any difference as all Chelmsford's appeals fell on deaf ears.

And in all honesty I didn't really care as I had been in the offices of a national newspaper in Fleet Street at the heart of the country's newspaper business and that was exciting enough even though I didn't actually see any reporters running about in raincoats and trilby hats. Who knew that six year later I would find myself working full time in the so-called ;street of shame' that was home to the *Express*, *Telegraph*, *Times*, *News of The World*, and *Mail* before they all moved out to pastures new.

In addition to the Andrews family, my colleagues at the *Essex Chronicle* and its sister Tuesday paper the Chelmsford Newsman included new-ish reporter Lou Cummins, a local Grammar school boy who was a bit older than me, obsessed with rugby (I think he was a regular in Chelmsford's 3rd XV) and keen on climbing the town's not so very tall social ladder.

The chief news reporter was Stuart Birch, a bespectacled man who had an impressive Mini Cooper plus an advanced driving licence, something which cropped up regularly in any conversation. As I didn't drive I didn't much care and when he did drive me anywhere, it seemed the whole 'advanced' thing seemed to be about going very fast while talking incessantly about the traffic and getting as close to other vehicles as possible without actually hitting them which, to his credit and my relief, he managed to do.

Alongside him was Freddie Tapp who could well have been at the *Chronicle* since the day it started. He was old and extremely fat but was blessed with the best chuckling laugh ever and was prone to bursting into fits of giggles at things only he found funny. Dressed in either a tweed suit and waistcoat or a white linen jacket, he was left to write a regular column of his own thoughts and also go through the copy which came in from some of the paper's weekly columnists such as James Wentworth Day and Sir John Elliott, plus P.R. Hayward's Farm Chat.

Apparently all these people lived in Essex and were important, but sad to say I never actually met or even caught sight of any of them. Wentworth Day wrote about anything and everything from education, sport and the future of water weasels in Essex to politics which might have been his specialist subject as he was what was known as a 'High Tory' - a traditional Conservative with a fancy for the landed gentry and aristocracy. Apparently he had been a fan of the Italian dictator Mussolini but had his doubts about Adolf Hitler which was good to know.

Cub reporters together: Lou Cummins (right) and me, obviously going somewhere important in our matching Sunday best

While Hayward was a genuine Essex farmer, Elliott was the former head of the Thomas Cook travel company and he was happy to share with our readers his views on world travel (obviously), politics and sport including a memorable feature on the difference between European and Latin sportsmen and women – no sexism but just a touch of racism.

Jane Hemmings was the paper's link with the County set; she wore twin sets and pearls, along with big fancy spectacles, and went on about hunts and point-to-point races and regularly brought her floppy-eared basset hound into the office. These were not my sort of people although Cummins and I became friends as we set about learning our new trade together, and Tapp was both kind and the first real eccentric I had ever come across. To his eternal credit he was also well ahead of the game as in March 1965 he wrote that 'City status must come to fast expanding Chelmsford' and for those of us (mainly me) who thought a cathedral and a football team called City was enough, it came as a surprise to realise that Chelmsford was simply a town.

While Tapp explained that "few towns in the south east have been undergoing such a rapid process of growth and development" he would have been disappointed that the whole 'City' thing took so long and eventually only came about as part of Queen Elizabeth's Diamond Jubilee celebrations in 2012.

We all sat in one long office with Andrews and Spargo at the top facing their underlings with their two desks separated by about a yard. We were all at desks that formed a square with two people on either side facing each other while Birch sat in the back row on his own. Close to him, alongside the picture window that ran for half the length of the room was the sports desk (actually two desks pushed

together) where sports editor Bernard Webber and his assistant Martin Rogers focussed on Chelmsford City, Colchester United (I never quite understood this as we were
a Chelmsford paper although I later learned that Webber
lived near Colchester) plus Essex county cricket and assorted local teams and sports including rugby, speedway, tennis (lawn and table), rallying and scrambling.

Webber was a gambling man but it took me a while to
work out that the frequent phone calls he made in hushed
tones during the day were to his bookmaker. It was all new
to me as I'd never gambled and didn't understand why he
was saying things like "Barbarian Bill, Newbury 2.30" ten
bob each way" Did horses run one way and then the other?
Whatever they were doing, I never knew if he ever won
as there were never any celebrations or trips to the pub to
spend any ill-gotten gains.

Martin Rogers on the other hand was a speedway nut
who spent most of his free time running and promoting
speedway teams and races, in particular in Kings Lynn. He
was also, obviously for a sports writer, a football fan and
although he wasn't fit to play – 30 fags a day and an ob-
session with cleanliness made him an unlikely full back or
centre forward – he did run, manage and finance a local
team called St Margarets.

The club was based in the village of Leaden Roding (Rogers lived in High Roding but as I was to discover there
were loads of Rodings) and anybody who worked at the
Chronicle and could kick a ball was recruited to play for
him. I was persuaded to join first his Sunday team and then
his Saturday XI and regularly played with at least four or
five blokes from the print room and even captained one
team to a glorious cup semi-final defeat.

Up at the front of the office, the desks of Ken Andrews

and Josie Spargo, a tall, thin, short sighted, blonde lady who smoked menthol cigarettes continuously, backed onto a pair of glass double doors which opened onto a very small balcony. Throughout the day, Andrews and Spargo passed secret notes to each other like naughty school kids and we, who sat facing them, watched with amusement at this bizarre and cumbersome way to run what we assumed was an illicit affair.

And it became an embarrassment when Andrews junior was around although fortunately he faced me across a desk with his back to his dad and his fancy piece. Their behaviour was a regular topic for gossip and while Hemmings, the only other woman in the office, tried to dampen the flames, we all chatted and chuckled while keeping our heads down.

On a regular daily basis the editor and his assistant would get up, leave the office, at carefully spaced intervals of about three minutes, and go off either in his impressive Rover or her bizarre Metropolitan car which was half white and half yellow with a white soft top and bright yellow wheels - not the ideal car for a secret liaison we all thought...

Where did they go, what did they do? None of those who had a car – and that didn't include me - had the balls to follow them and find out. I think we all knew well enough what was going on but had the good sense to keep quiet about it. But then again maybe we were all wrong and they were ahead of their time in holding in-depth, one-on-one editorial policy briefings in a secluded field or car park.

Chapter 3

SUITED AND 'BEATLE' BOOTED

On my first day I was given the ten-bob tour of the *Chronicle* which involved a walk down the corridor towards the canteen, past the advertising department which had bright, light offices overlooking the main road. Then it was down the stairs and through reception where a very large, scary spinster called Miss Mundy was on guard, overseeing who came in and went out while she dealt with reams of paperwork.

Within just a few weeks, I came to realise that she was hugely important in the scheme of things as she dealt with our pittance of a weekly wage plus any minor expenses – both of which were handed over as cash in brown envelopes. She was also in charge of supplies; the treasure cupboard of stationery items which were the essential tools of our trade.

You had to go to this formidable lady to get a notebook (ones that always flipped open upwards and consequently took up less space), biros (only blue BIC with the delightfully chewable top were on offer) and pencils although you had to supply your own pencil sharpener and rubber. These were the things we needed to go out and collect "all the news that's fit to print" in the words of *New York Times* owner Adolph Ochs.

On the occasion of Miss Elsie Mundy's 40th anniversary as chief cashier with the paper, an article ran which accurately described her as an "authority on what goes on inside the *Chronicle*." And even though she was quite intimidating and viewed anything untoward that went on amongst us young people as a personal attack on her high moral standards (she was a Girl Guide leader), she did show me an unexpected moment of generosity.

I had developed a fascination with antique shops – especially one in Broomfield Road – where I bought what even I can only describe as a bizarre collection of objets d'art or useless crap. There was a four foot long stuffed crocodile, a glass case of stuffed birds (including one eating a field mouse ... also stuffed), Victorian mourning rings and bracelets (the ones with hair in them), an ornate ceremonial Gurkha curved machete known as a kukri and an African assegai or spear.

These were the days when you could wander around a busy suburban town with a six foot spear in your hand and go unnoticed and untroubled by the local fuzz. The shop certainly didn't bother to wrap it and I was pretty cocksure of myself as I was 'tooled up' in the most exotic fashion.

I took it into a local coffee bar where one of the co-owners decided to test it out by throwing it at – and through – the wooden door to the toilet which luckily was vacant at the time. When I got back to the office, Miss Mundy was on watch and was fascinated by my latest purchase. The conversation then moved on to cover my small collection of weapons – I also had an American WWI Remington bay-onet which we had found in the garden of our house in Widford.

I learned later that as no US servicemen were ever sta-tioned anywhere near Chelmsford during the 1914-1918 war, it was probably left in our garden, when it was just a field close to Hylands House, which was used as a milit-ary hospital during the war, by a British soldier who had swapped it or 'borrowed' it from one his American brothers in arms.

Miss Mundy then opened up to me about her brother who had served with the British army in India and brought back with him a bamboo walking cane which doubled as a pretty terrifying sword stick plus a serving Gurkha's kukri which came without any inlays or flashiness. And then the very next day she presented them both to me as a gift and I was so moved that I toyed with the idea of calling her Elsie but decided better of it.

The ground floor at the *Chronicle* also housed the readers' rooms and these people were a complete mystery to me. Apparently these men and women, most of whom wore spectacles with very thick what were called 'milk bottle' lenses, spent their days assiduously reading all the copy generated upstairs by us journos, and fact-checking it to make sure nobody got their arse sued.

From there it was on to the print floor where the 'inkies' as they were known, turned the words we had typed on sheets of A5 paper not much bigger than a piece of toilet paper (some would say it was right size for some of the crap we wrote) into lines of hot metal type which were laid out in individual trays or blocks, each the size of a page of the tabloid *Chronicle* as opposed to our broadsheet rival the *Weekly News*.

The printers followed a design or layout sent down from editorial showing which stories went on which page and with which headline and photograph. Anyone who wants or needs to know more about type sizes, typefaces and type setting should get a copy of Allen Hutt's book *Newspaper Design*, which was published in 1960. My father gave me the book as a present somewhere in the mid-sixties although I would probably rather have had a copy of the latest Beatles LP. Interestingly I still have both the book and all the Beatles albums.

In 1964 the so-called press room where the actual printing of the newspapers took place was not in the new *Chronicle* building. It wasn't until 1967, when the paper also introduced new page layouts and type-faces, that new web-offset presses, apparently costing £100,000, rolled into Westway. This was fancy, modern, clean technology involving a continuous roll of paper that was cut and folded after printing, and this advance was closely followed by 'paste-up' where pages previously set in hot metal were now produced as 'cold type' on photographic paper that was then cut and pasted to create a page which became film in some magical way.

To a non-mechanical young man who had trouble assembling a bicycle pump, the old rotary presses were without doubt one of the most overwhelming yet still impressive (and incredibly noisy) things I had witnessed in my short life. Two huge cylinders made up the actual press – one with plates containing the metal print and one offering up the paper – and they rotated (this was why it was called a rotary press) in opposite directions for a while before amazingly spewing out a finished newspaper.

The impressive new presses ran with a continuous roll of paper which produced 40,000 printed pages an hour, which were somehow cut after printing and then folded and bound as a newspaper. And to think that, despite all this technology, within a day or two it would be wrapped around a piece of cod and six penn'orth of chips ... c'est la vie I suppose.

Even though I played football with some of the lads who worked in the print room – and it was all men – there was an invisible barrier between us whenever we journalists went down on the 'stone' (the name given to the area where the newspaper was laid out for printing as it used to be done on a stone) and it was all to do with unions. We scribes, as we liked to call ourselves, were members of either the National Union of Journalists (NUJ) or the Institute of Journalists (IOJ) while the compositors who set and arranged the type were members of (wait for it) the snappily named National Society of Operative Printers & Assistants (NATSOPA).

As this was years before Rupert Murdoch took on – and some say destroyed - the print unions at his plant in Wapping in East London, there were still strict rules about who could and couldn't touch the 'hot metal' when the page was being laid out. Editorial staff had to stand aside and, while we could chat to the lay out man, we were never, never, ever allowed to touch a single piece of metal type or even pick up the metal rule which measured the column widths in 'ems' (which was a term taken from the width of the letter 'm') and indicated the width of a newspaper column. It reminded me of the Coasters hit 'Poison Ivy' – "you can look but you better not touch."

Such treacherous action on our part would result in the print shop's union chief being called into action to issue a severe warning and, if that warning wasn't heeded, then the works manager – in this case an ex-RAF hero of Bomber Command called Ralph Tyrrell, who ran his print shop with

all the efficiency of a wartime operation - would be called
into play to decide if strike action was necessary. He was
assisted by Jack Carrington who was ramrod straight and
boasted one of the finest RAF handlebar moustaches I'd
ever seen. It was odd to learn later that he had never gone
to war but joined the paper aged 15 in 1942.

While I don't recall there ever being a strike at the *Chronicle* during my time – and most minor misdemeanours on
the part of us journalists were overlooked by the printers
- the threat was always there, hanging like the sword of
Damocles over any of us who dared touch the type or lift
a metal rule.

Generally the relationship between writers and printers
was pretty good humoured. We shared a canteen, played in
combined *Chronicle* football and cricket teams and we upstairs even showed appropriate sympathy for those downstairs when a lad called Alan was rushed to hospital after
getting his penis caught in his trouser zip. He told me later
that in hospital he was seen to by a very business-like and
unsympathetic nurse whose remedy involved a hefty yank
on the zip and the application of some highly pungent and
powerful stinging liquid to his blood-stained and damaged
private part.

On the ground floor of the office, with a picture window
overlooking a bit of mangy grass, was the photographic department complete with a dark room for processing photos
in double-quick time. Under the leadership of keen boat-
ing enthusiast Geoff Baker, Ray Horsnall, a former navy
submariner who still suffered some stressful mental issues
from spending days or months under water in a tin can,
and Tony Tween, completed the paper's trio of 'snappers.'

Tween, who was the youngest and quietest of the photo
threesome and went on to become a minister in a local

church, took to calling me, for some inexplicable reason, Brian Boru, after the 11th century King of Ireland. Still it was slightly better than my grammar school nickname of 'Suv', a clumsy abbreviation of the name Southall and not half as clever as the name given to my mate Alan Westwood who was known as 'Ho'.

The photographers managed their own diary with some input from the editorial nobs in order to ensure that there were pictures to go with the stories, but in the main they did their own thing. This ranged from snapping attractive young ladies with ambitions to enter and win local beauty contests to rushing out at a moment's notice to get to a road accident or fire.

Working closely with these three 'snappers' often meant going out with them to one of the 'incidents' that they had heard about on the police wave bands they tuned to on the radio in their secret dark room area. It was illegal to listen-in to these police messages but nobody on the paper was ever going to make an issue of it as the result was often an exciting if horrific or tragic image of an accident or fire.

Of course, the paper never printed the worst of these shots, settling for a picture of a wrecked vehicle or burnt out building which never featured dead or badly injured people. But these sorts of events put some pressure on us reporters as we then had to do the 'follow up' and get details of the people involved.

If there was a fatality we had to get an address from the police, fire brigade or ambulance crew and then pay the family a visit and hope to come back with a quote and, even better, a photo of the deceased. This was never a task any of us relished but bizarrely we received very little abuse from relatives and they would, more often than not, give us a picture of their loved one to go with the report.

Often the photographers would arrive at the most grue-some events before the ambulance or police and although the gory real life up close and personal photos never made it into the paper, I would occasionally get a private viewing in the dark room of the pictures that were not fit to print … and it was an eye-opening experience in a truly gruesome way.

Similarly, but on a happier note, they would also show off the more revealing poses some of the hopeful young ladies adopted to get on the right side of a smooth talking snapper. This was way before the *Sun's* controversial Page 3 topless pin-up pictures but girls posing provocatively was a centuries old subject for painters and photographers and what I witnessed in the dark room was 'all in the best pos-sible taste' and seen simply as a little bit saucy.

An added fascination for me was the fact that I knew a good number of the young ladies featured in these pho-tos as they were girls 'about town' who were regulars in coffee bars and at local dances but, disappointingly and some would say surprisingly, none of them ever fell for the charms of a certain trainee reporter.

Most of these glamour shots were taken by Ray Horsnall who, despite being short, balding and overweight, had a knack of persuading the prettiest girls in the area to pose for a weekly pin-up photo which was published for the flimsiest of editorial reasons. The ladies wore skimpy tops and short skirts, which showed off quite a lot of cleavage and stocking tops, while holding a cricket bat to launch the cricket season, draped over a bale of hay to coincide with harvesting or sitting astride a motor bike at some scramble meet.

There was a weekly editorial meeting of sorts during which, in my early days, I just sat and listened and took no active part – after all I didn't really know what was going on. Andrews and Spargo would assign various jobs to the reporters with Cummins and me usually getting the rough end of the stick.

We were sent to cover carnivals, bazaars, fetes, amateur plays and given publicity hand-outs to turn into copy, mainly for Tuesday's *Newsman* which had just a couple of pages of weekend news alongside sports coverage. The rest of the paper was made up with reviews of the films on locally, plus assorted gardening pieces and clothing and food items which made up the regular "Fashion & Cookery" column for "our feminine readers." This was written by somebody called June Patricia who, as there was nobody of that name on the paper, I guessed to be either (or both) Spargo or Hemmings.

The odd thing about the *Chronicle's* Tuesday paper was the confusion caused locally by its name. Throughout the 1940s and 1950s it had been called the Newsman Herald after being launched earlier as the *Essex Newsman Herald*. However by the time I joined it had officially become the *Chelmsford Newsman* although it never mattered what name was on the masthead as it was always simply known as the *Newsman*.

Whether, back in the sixties, I was working for the *Chronicle*, the *Herald* or the *Newsman*, I don't recall being given any instructions about a dress code but it was the norm for every bloke to wear a shirt and tie and either a suit or jacket and smart trousers. There were no jeans, t-shirts or open necked holiday shirts and at least looking the part of a professional in court was de rigueur – after all even the accused usually turned up to court in their best gear in an effort to convince the bench that they might just be innocent.

For a lad who later in life would sport long flowing shoulder-length locks – sometimes permed, sometimes straight (it was rock 'n' roll after all) – the early to mid-sixties was a time for experimentation with hair. The Beatles and The Rolling Stones had arrived with what was considered to be outrageously long hair although in fact it just about covered the tops of their ears. It was the style I opted for and got away with, despite my father's protests. In fact looking back my hair was no longer than George Harrison's on the cover of the *With The Beatles album* – and you can see most of his ears.

The fact that George's ears are poking out on that album sleeve came up a few years back in a conversation I had with the young man who played Harrison in the tribute act the Bootleg Beatles - and it showed how committed these boys were to their role as Beatle look-alikes. He told me that in order to get the right 'look' when they were playing songs from that early sixties period he always tucked a bit of sponge or tissue under the wig cap to push his ears out. Apparently the fans made a real fuss if everything wasn't as it should be with the 'Fab Four' impersonators.

I was also told that the man who 'played' John Lennon as a right handed guitarist in the band, looked so much like Paul McCartney that he was persuaded to change persona and learn to become a left-handed bass player. The things people do for their art.

My Beatles-style Cuban-heeled boots – bought in the famous Anello & Davide shop in Covent Garden where The Beatles also shopped – were smart enough and I was all set – literally suited and booted - to take on the cream of Chelmsford's councils, committees, companies and courts. The rules were thankfully bent in the evenings or at weekends if you were covering a carnival or bazaar or reviewing something which usually took place in a darkened auditorium. Then a casual shirt or roll neck jumper with casual slacks, which I often teamed up with a rather dashing real suede jacket, (something I bought after seeing the cover of Bob Dylan's 1964 album *The Freewheelin' Bob Dylan*) was deemed OK, but you could never be seen in the office without a shirt and tie.

I do recall a period when Lou Cummins and I (and I think it was his idea) opted for collarless shirts in an array of bright colours which were worn with a stiff, white starched collar held at the neck with a stud. They were uncomfortable, always required a tie and consequently couldn't be loosened to let in some air … God knows who we were trying to impress but it certainly wasn't my mother who was left with the job of starching the collars.

Chapter 4

IF THE CAPS FIT

Among the numerous fetes I was assigned to cover –
and I assume I got a lift from a photographer – was one
in nearby Woodham Mortimer in the grounds of local businessman Alan Brush's home. He was big in aggregates and
usually referred to as a 'gravel millionaire' and his house,
Woodham Mortimer Place on the road between Chelmsford and Maldon, was the venue for the local village fete in
August 1965 when pop singer Julie Rogers performed the
ribbon cutting.

She had hit number three in the UK charts a year earlier
with 'The Wedding' – which went on to sell a million copies
worldwide – but it was her only top ten hit and here she
was, just a year later, opening a fete in a tiny village with a
population of less than 500. The paper ran a caption story
which explained that she had just flown in all the way from
Bournemouth and she told me exclusively (I was the only
reporter there) that she was sorry she couldn't stay all afternoon but she had to get back to Bournemouth for her
evening appearance.

I didn't for a moment think 'how the mighty have fallen'

(I wasn't really old enough to be a true cynic) but was more than happy to be up close and almost personal with this glamorous pop singer - and she was a beauty - and have the chance for a brief chat before Mr Brush whisked her inside his mansion for afternoon tea. It was an early brush (geddit?) with the world of pop music and, no matter how un-hip it was, I really rather liked it.

Looking back it was amazing how many celebs (and these were genuine celebrities not modern day one made-up for TV) came to town to open garages, shops, fetes or attend school prize-givings. There was *Avengers* star Patrick McNee, pop sensation Cliff Richard, soccer legends Jimmy Greaves and Billy Wright, celebrated actor Oliver Reed, TV host Cathy McGowan and boxing champion Henry Cooper. It was obvious even to a greenhorn like me that back then there must have been some sort of celebrity hot line like "book a star" or "we have proper celebs for you."

Pop star Julie Rogers, who I met at a fete in a tiny Essex village in 1965

None of this was exactly Rudyard Kipling or Mark Twain I grant you, but it was miles better than not filling in forms about ships at sea. In fact my own reading matter around this time was nothing more classical than the celebrated American detective novels of Mickey Spillane and his hero Mike Hammer. I also read the *Daily Mirror* as it was the newspaper of choice for my father who was a Labour supporter (but not necessarily a socialist) and also 'father' or head of the local NUJ chapel.

The *Mirror* – and its sister *Sunday Mirror* – boasted some of the finest sports writers of the day in the form of Peter Wilson, Frank McGhee and Ken Jones plus somebody who wrote under the name Cassandra and turned out to be called William Connor (what was all that about I wondered) and the wonderful Andy Capp cartoons created by Reg Smythe.

And while these genuine newspaper legends were being read and enjoyed by over five and a half million people (the world's largest circulation) I was busy producing wedding and funeral reports from the *Essex Chronicle*'s official "matches and dispatches" forms which arrived from families or undertakers. The only good news was that we didn't have to go to either the weddings or the funerals.

This was a time when the *Chronicle* was regularly producing either 48 or 56 page editions which sold for 4d (under 2p) and included columns of local wills so people could work out who had left what to whom. There was also a page of official marriage, birth and death announcements where readers would get a 12 word message for 3s (15p) with every six words or fewer costing an extra 1s 6d (7p).

The highlight of the day for the junior staff came first thing in the morning when two of us wannabe journos – usually Cummins and me in his battered VW Beetle - would call at the ambulance, fire and police stations to get details of any overnight activity. Nothing was on-line in those days, nobody filmed things and sent in images and rarely did the public think to call their local rag to tell them who was doing what to whom. The police might have had paid informants but we didn't.

These daily calls resulted in us collecting information about events that ambulances or fire engines were called to and deciding whether they were serious enough to follow up. As intrepid reporters we weren't much interested in cats stuck up trees or drunks falling over and breaking a bone or two; we wanted hard news about death and destruction, arson and armed robbery, car crashes and big time crime in and around the Chelmsford area.

Often these stories ended up as little more than a paragraph about a car theft on Melbourne Estate, shoplifting from a corner shop in Springfield, a minor punch-up outside a pub along Broomfield Road. But it was all news and it came from a healthy, respectful relationship between the paper and the three main emergency services. In return each week we would drop off a dozen or so free copies of the paper at the three stations.

Chelmsford's Tardis-like police station sat on the corner of New Street and Waterloo Lane. It was an odd, ugly and probably Victorian building with a sort of Rapunzel spire and boasted half a dozen cells out back across a small courtyard, plus a tunnel which ran underground to the local Shire Hall where the courts sat each week. It still stands in Chelmsford today with a Grade II Listing and a more recent potted history as a restaurant and assorted bars.

Our regular contact was the desk sergeant who was the nearest thing we had to George Dixon of *Dixon of Dock Green* fame and, like the amiable TV character, his days of going out to pursue villains in a high speed chase – with or without a car – were long behind him. He was best suited to overseeing the front office and information desk with just the right mix of good humour, sarcasm and disdain for us young whipper-snappers.

The information that came from the ambulance and fire stations was, in all honesty, not earth shattering; I came to realise that unless there was a multi-car pile-up or major house or factory fire, they didn't offer much in the way of hard news. The police, however, were the keepers of all the news that we wanted to print and while the sarge and his oppos gave us just the bare bones of the previous night's events as they appeared in his incident book, they did include all the road crashes and blazing infernos alongside break-ins, burglaries, punch-ups and robberies.

I don't recall the actual size of the editorial office at the *Essex Chronicle* in feet and inches but it was presumably custom-built for the task in 1964 when the paper moved into the new Westway building from its long-time but rather shoddy and cramped offices in the town's High Street. The new building, designed by local architects Stanley Bragg, was a modern typical 1960s flat-roofed monstrosity with few redeeming features, which arrived just as the *Chronicle* notched up its double century and a weekly circulation of around 40,000.

With its polystyrene ceiling tiles (later to become popular with health freaks under the guise of rice cakes) and constantly buzzing fluorescent lighting strips, the office was home to around a dozen journalists during my time and it was a tight squeeze, which wasn't made any easier or more comfortable by the half-a-dozen smokers who expelled more smoke than a test lab full of cigarette-smoking monkeys.

There weren't such things as smoke-free zones anywhere

in the building as printers also smoked as they went about their business and the advertising staff did much the same. I had become a Tom Thumb small cigar man while, oddly, I don't think any of the three photographers ever smoked even as they snapped the most horrifying scenes.

This was when I came face-to-face for the first time with people from previously distant religions and races. I wasn't naïve - after all I was a child of sixties - and had read *Lady Chatterley's Lover*, seen Jayne Mansfield strutting all her stuff in *The Girl Can't Help It* and spotted the almost topless dancers in Cliff Richard's *Expresso Bongo*.

I'd also bought records by black American singers such as Ray Charles and Fats Domino, knew all about Sammy Davis Jnr and Harry Belafonte, had seen British Guyanese calypso singer Cy Grant on the Tonight TV show in the late 1950s and watched the film *A Kid For Two Farthings* with its strong Jewish influence and David Kossoff in a starring role. But I had only got up close and personal with citizens of the British Isles and didn't mind even if they came from Scotland, Wales or Northern Ireland.

At junior school there was a kid with an even stranger accent than my West Midland twang which I brought with me when we moved from Kidderminster. He was from New Zealand, had traces of Maori in his make-up and was the colour of a walnut shell.

Then at my mixed grammar school there was a girl who had come from South Africa, complete with the weirdest accent I'd ever heard and skin the colour of a very well-tanned holidaymaker.

And then, with skin as white as a fine china cup and without any trace of an accent, there arrived at the *Chronicle* a new reporter called Peter who was Jewish. He was polite and resourceful – no different to loads of young blokes

I knew around town – except that he got some perks I was not aware of. He had special holidays which we didn't get and then enjoyed our special holidays as well. Lucky bugger I thought. He didn't stay with the paper for long but his penchant for wearing the latest Hush Puppy shoes is the thing I remember most clearly. Maybe it stuck with me because I favoured the Beatles-inspired Chelsea boot.

Then there was John who is best described as a cross between the Fifties comedian Jimmy James and Mick Jagger. I had no idea how old he was – anywhere between 40 and 70 was my best guess – but was always taken with his face which was creased like a well-worn linen shirt. It was what they called 'lived-in' (except most people would have moved out years ago) and always put me in mind of veteran jazz singer George Melly's wonderful line about Mick Jagger when he remarked on the singer's famously lined face. When Jagger explained that they were laughter lines, Melly replied. "Nothing that's funny."

Our John was a veteran journalist, a hack of the highest order who had been round the block more than a few times since he left his native county somewhere t'up north. He smoked incessantly and could blow smoke out of both sides of mouth with the cigarette still clenched between his lips. His voice was testament to his 40 (maybe 50) a day habit and a penchant for whisky, and whenever I looked at him I saw what a lifetime chasing down a story could do for you. Not quite washed up – he could still turn a phrase and recount a good tale – but living alone in digs, on a diet of ciggies and booze and not sure how long he was going to stay at this or any other particular job. And sure enough he moved on just as suddenly as he arrived, but without any of the glamour or mystery of a comic book hero.

Dick was the first black man I ever worked alongside. He

was the van delivery driver who drove from the paper's Westway offices into the centre of Chelmsford where there was a small *Chronicle* office which was woman-ed by three ladies who took in adverts, death notices, wedding forms and orders for photographs. One of them was about my age, another was probably in her late thirties and the other was even older than that.

This tiny office – now a sandwich bar in Duke Street – became a hideaway for any of us who were covering the courts or afternoon meetings as we hunkered down in the back room and pinched instant coffee and biscuits. There was a typewriter so we could actually do some work and also a telephone which allowed us to phone copy through to the head office, but mainly it served as a getaway and, on a good day, the ladies would tell the odd white lie about our whereabouts to keep the bosses off our young backs.

When any of us journalists who didn't have a car, or those who did but didn't want to park for hours in the town centre, needed to go into Chelmsford we scrounged a lift with Dick who was tall and thin, with what little hair he had plastered down with a slightly pungent hair grease. As far I was concerned he must have come from a far off exotic land because he was the colour of dark chocolate, but disappointingly the only accent he had was a mix of Essex and East London without any hint of what I assumed to be African, West Indian or Indian ... which I would have known back then as 'foreign'.

Dick was always polite but punctuality was his watch word and if you wanted a lift you had to be ready at his appointed times and if there was more than one of us who wanted a ride into town, somebody had to go in the back of the windowless van with reams of paper and sacks of mail – and usually it was the newest kid on the block.

As I got into the routine of life as a journalist, well a very junior cub reporter (why cub and not kitten or pup I occasionally asked but satisfied myself that it was more 'butch' than a young cat or dog), I came to realise it was a combination of morning station calls, followed by chasing the more exciting stories that came out of the round-up, and then maybe settling into the boring routine of writing a bunch of wedding reports or checking through a funeral report to see if the deceased was important or notorious enough to warrant a proper obituary.

I wasn't really let out on my own for a few weeks as I learnt the ropes, mastered the mechanics of my allotted ancient office typewriter, which I swiftly replaced with my own portable Olivetti, and worked on my telephone manner – a necessity when calling distressed parents, outraged council officials, smarmy big company spokespeople, enthusiastic teachers or charity workers. They all had either a story to tell or were upset about a story already told and as 'their local paper' we had a major role to play. I learnt that you had to get the details right, make sure the quotes were accurate and, most important of all, spell people's names correctly and never get their age wrong.

There was nothing worse, I came to realise, than mentioning somebody in a news story or feature and misspelling their name. It was the sin of all sins, alongside adding ten years to a person's age – 24 could easily become 34 with a simple slip of your typing finger and no sub editor would ever spot the error.

Even after 40 years, I know that typing errors are just as easy to make on a computer keyboard and I made my biggest faux pas in this area when, in 2006, I wrote a book called *Northern Songs*, about The Beatles' music publishing empire. The book included a photograph of Michael Jackson (who bought all the Lennon/McCartney songs) and his lawyer at the attorney's wedding. The photo was kindly loaned to us by the lawyer and I managed (thanks to my trusty two-fingered typing style) to transcribe the year of the wedding to make it 1978 instead of 1987. No great damage done but I had to hang my head and send profuse apologies across the water to Los Angeles.

Ken Andrews and Josie Spargo were the main sub editors (or subs as they were known) while Jane Hemmings and Stuart Birch, the most senior staff members, stepped up as first reserves when needed. There was a house style that we all had to follow when typing up a story and it involved what went in italics, what had 'single' or "double" quotation marks, which words might need to be CAPPED UP and whether companies such as Marconi or Hoffman were singular or plural.

Then there were the sort of unwritten rules of the game which were pressed home every time you offered up a story. If it involved a person doing anything - good or bad – the first paragraph had to identify them (not always with their name, that could wait until the second para), give their age, where they came from and what had happened. In the second para you got into the guts of the story.

"A 21 year old man from South Hanningfield was taken into custody by Chelmsford Police on Monday morning accused of stealing a trumpet and playing it badly outside his local public house.

"Bill Bloggs, of Back Street, was arrested at around 2am as he left the Limping Donkey after neighbours complained that they could not recognise any of the tunes he was playing in the pub car park." Everything you need to know in two paragraphs.

With this in mind my copy was gone through with a fine-tooth comb and subbed by those who knew better than me. If they scribbled just a few corrections on it, in addition to marking the type size, column width and identifying the page it was to go on, I was relieved to have got it right or at least nearly right.

There were occasions, however, when I was called up and given a lesson in how the story should read and, even worse, given the whole thing back to do again. There was an element of being back at school, but these were lessons to be learned. However, I did wonder whether Shakespeare had a sub who went through his plays and poems with a fine quill.

When our copy, which was always typed up with three sheets of white paper and two sheets of carbon paper in between, was deemed fit to print it went down a chute from the editorial office to the print department where it was 'processed' by the readers, typesetters and printers before becoming part of the paper and ultimately read by thousands before then being used as firelighter, tossed in the garbage or used as cat litter. Such was often the destiny of great prose!

Chapter 5

THE STORY OF O

As a teenager in the swinging sixties – I was still only about 17 years old – my interests focussed on the three subjects that were on the minds of almost every adolescent male: football, pop music and girls OR girls, football and pop music OR pop music, girls and football. The order wasn't important as it always depended on the circumstances.

If it was a Sunday morning match then footie took precedence, if it was a new record by The Beatles, The Stones or The Who then that had to be chased down while, if there was a chance of getting a date for a trip to the pictures, then that became the focus of attention along with a bath, hair wash and a search for pimples to be exploded; shaving was still some way off.

The *Chronicle* covered what passed for The Arts in Chelmsford with reviews of plays and shows at the town's Civic Theatre which opened in 1962 and was designed in true sixties style – serviceable with just a hint of flash. Local productions by amateur dramatic and operatic societies usually went on at the cavernous Regent cinema cum theatre while there was the never-ending cycle of village and school efforts that we covered on a very ad hoc basis.

If the performance was by a grammar school (remember we had three) or in a village where someone important lived, then usually somebody on the paper was sent along and the best intentioned amateur efforts at *King Lear, Aladdin* or *The Mousetrap* would get a review ... and it always had to be as positive as possible otherwise there would repercussions.

You never gave an amateur production a real roasting but instead went down the route of finding something, anything, complimentary to say.

If a hall was half empty you said it was half full and if you hated every minute of it, you mentioned that the audience (usually the local villagers, teachers, parents or children) loved every minute.

And there were always useful phrases you could use and one of them stayed with me into my long association with Cliff Richard. In 1996 I went to see him in the musical *Wuthering Heights* when he played a less than convincing Heathcliff in what was an all-round disappointing evening's entertainment which one critic cleverly described as "living dull."

When we got together backstage and Cliff asked me what I thought, I very convincingly, and with a straight face, told him "I've never seen anything like it." And I hadn't, but fortunately he took it the wrong way – as a compliment!

I was never asked to review any of the professional things that went on at the Civic as those were left to Hemmings who was the Arts correspondent, although Cummins stood in when she was away.

I also never got to cast an eye over the local operatic efforts (thank God!) or the often lavish amateur dramatic presentations, but I was handed a few village and school plays and one of them almost got me the sack.

It was something put on a by a school in Springfield and I went along with an old school mate who insisted on making cruel and – it has to be said – very funny asides about what was going on onstage. Unfortunately he was overheard by the headmaster who was equally upset at my giggling and chose to report me to big boss man Handley.

I was called in to see him and made to explain myself and luckily was able to talk my way out of it by blaming my anonymous school chum and sending a letter of grovelling apology to the school. I left his office with an official warning on my record, but the good news was that I was now well down the list when it came to reviewing drama of any sort.

There were, however, films to be reviewed and this was done for the *Newsman*. What was most fascinating and in some way satisfying was that we often reviewed the films without seeing them. We were writing our critiques usually on a Friday or during the odd Saturday morning shift while the films actually opened on the following Sunday or Monday.

But courtesy of the film companies' publicity hand-outs and reviews in the national press we were able to cobble together some wonderfully bland and (again) usually favourable reviews, and, in return for not slagging off something we'd never seen, we got free entry to the town's four local cinemas.

These 'freebie' treats came from the Regent, Odeon, Select and Pavilion cinemas in the form of weekly cards which allowed two people to go once a week (not weekends) to each picture house. The girl at the cash desk ticked off the week and you saved yourself the few bob it normally cost to get in. Birch put himself in charge of these tickets as he oversaw the film review page and he handed them out to his colleagues like a monarch dispensing Maundy money at Easter. He knew they were a valuable commodity not to be handed out lightly and of course he always had first crack at the best films in the first (and sometimes only) week they were on.

There was a tall, bespectacled man in charge at the Odeon and he impressively but oddly always wore a dinner jacket and bow tie as if every show was a Royal Command Performance. He was known as Sir Jim and his glamorous assistant was a peroxide blonde of a certain age called Eve who would sometimes allow us apprentice scribes free entry even when we didn't have 'the pass'.

The smaller and slightly less salubrious Select and Pavilion cinemas were owned by local businessman George Watkins who was a dapper, silver-haired man with a trim moustache. Despite both of them being known as the 'flea pit', he ran them with a rod of iron and took exception to any unruly behaviour by the local yobs.

Back in 1956 when the controversial movie *Rock Around The Clock* came to his Select cinema in New Writtle Street, Watkins was so concerned that there might be a repetition of the rioting that had gone on in cinemas around the UK that he employed his own squad of vigilantes.

Under the headline "Riot squad is ready", the *Chronicle* described the movie as "the film that has set teenagers all over the country rioting, leaving a trail of wrecked cinemas" and Watkins' solution was to hire a six man 'army' under the leadership of a local boxer and ex-Coldstream Guardsman who promised "if there are any troublemakers we'll deal with them outside the cinema."

In the end there was no trouble at all, just a handful of

exuberant girls and boys harmlessly jiving in the aisles. However when I went there in the sixties Watkins was still determined to keep any hanky-panky to a minimum and his usherettes wandered up and down the aisles shining their torches on any overly amorous activities, making sure nothing got out of hand ... or in hand if you prefer.

Chelmsford's cinemas flourished throughout the sixties but by 1992 all four of them had closed down with both the Select and Pavilion eventually being demolished to make way for flats while the Odeon was turned into a multi-story car park in Baddow Road. Only the Regent remains as a bar, having also been a bingo hall, in the original 1913 Grade II listed building.

Alongside the cinemas, there were a couple of not really dangerous but slightly threatening coffee bars serving Chelmsford's, it has to be said, rather modest rival gangs of mods and rockers. The Long Bar in Baddow Road was an appropriately named long thin L-shaped café where the rockers parked their noisy motor bikes in the street and then took espresso 'frothy' coffee, or perhaps a glass of milk or maybe a cola – both Coke and Pepsi were around back then.

However if you were not clad in leathers and jeans and didn't have your hair greased into a mighty quiff – and some bordered on the gravity defying - it was not a place you went into simply out of mild curiosity. Things often erupted into a half-hearted punch-up thanks to an over-long stare or a whispered wrong word. These guys and gals were sensitive souls and took exception to 'outsiders'.

Meanwhile, the Orpheus in New London Road became home to the town's mod community. Situated in a base-ment, the entrance to the stairs lay between a men's tail-ors and the Chelmsford Institute which was home to the offices of the Norwich Union Insurance company. Presumably named with a nod to Offenbach's comic opera *Orpheus In The Underworld* – although, if I was anything to go by, the reference was lost on most of us who trudged down the narrow staircase – the 'O' was my hideout of choice.

Being a mod, and I had a lot friends who were but, surprise, surprise none who were rockers, was the order of the day for a whole bunch of teenagers and they proudly displayed their allegiance to the movement that loved soul, R&B and ska music alongside British bands like The Who and The Small Faces. Fur trimmed parkas were their fashion statement although few who wore them would have known, or cared, that they originated in the Canadian Arctic courtesy of the local Inuit people

Decorated with sewn on badges of bands or pop art symbols, parkas were worn over a shiny, sometimes two tone tonic suit that was cut to fit with a three button jacket and the ensemble was completed by a Vespa or Lambretta scooter which boasted a thin six foot aerial with a fake fox tail hanging from it. Cheaper to run and far more hip than a car, scooters still didn't come cheap with a Lambretta S.X, which, according the advertising blurb, gave you "SiX appeal and rocket like acceleration", costing £179 and an up market "jet set" Lambretta coming in at £216. The adverts also claimed they had "weather protection" (I never saw a roof on one) and could be parked in "the smallest of spaces with no worries about parking meters"

I wasn't on the paper when the mods and rockers set about each other on the beaches of Sussex, Kent and our very own Clacton and Southend during the Easter weekend in 1964 and I still don't really know for sure if any of the locals from the 'O' or the Long Bar were down at the seaside back then, but a selection of our more mouthy and aggressive local mods such as Dave, Mickey and Paul could well have been contenders. If they were there they never bragged about their day out at the seaside which was surprising as it would have earned them 'brownie' points among their peers.

While the Orpheus, with its great jukebox selection, was a popular hang-out and a happy refuge after a hard day's reporting, it never held gigs by the local bands who were fast emerging in the shadow of The Beatles, The Stones and The Kinks. The swinging sixties eventually arrived 'properly' in Chelmsford in the spring of 1964 when local wrestler Robert Archer (or Bob Anthony to give him his wrestling persona) began promoting pop shows at the Corn Exchange.

Using the banner 'Saturday Scene', the town's cavernous Corn Exchange, built in 1857, became home on a Saturday evening to an impressive who's who of the best of British pop. Featuring (appropriately) The Who and The Spencer Davis Group through to David Bowie and Jimi Hendrix plus a whole host of other acts in between, Saturday Scene was the place to be seen at the weekend. It cost six shillings (30p) to see The Who, Spencer Davis and Bowie but a massive 10 bob (50p) to see the emerging Hendrix in February 1967, just as his debut single Hey Joe was climbing the UK charts, and the same to enjoy Pink Floyd in September 1967.

I have to admit that I missed Hendrix's appearance as I was on holiday in Majorca with my mum - my father, being a sports editor, didn't take holidays during the football season. I know we flew out of Southend airport and spent probably no more than seven days in a hotel in the capital city of Palma and, although I didn't pay, I don't reckon it cost much more than £25 per person but I'm not sure what you got for your money back then by way of accommodation and meals.

I had my moments at the 'Saturday Scene'. And a good number of them were in the name of journalism and not just to do with trying to get off with any of the girls who danced around their handbags. The Corn Exchange was not a luxurious venue but fortunately it was no longer blessed with the heady aroma of pig muck and cow dung from the old market that had been held behind the building between 1880 and 1963.

There were a few seats dotted around the walls but no ventilation; it was hot, sweaty, smoky and dingy and even though it had no licence for alcohol it still managed to incite the odd moment of violence as blokes accused one another of eyeing up 'their birds' or some other minor disagreement ended with a bout of half-hearted fisticuffs.

It was also the location for ballroom dancing lessons which were held in an upstairs area and also regular Tuesday and Thursday wrestling matches which involved the stars of the day including Archer himself (sometimes in a tag team with his brother Chris), Johnny Apollo, Giant Anaconda and the future star of 1980s TV show *Auf Wiedersehen Pet*, Pat Roach. The match between Pietro Capello (supposedly from Italy) and Prince Kumadi (billed as hailing from West Africa) was billed as "An Outstanding Black v White Clash of the Giants."

And the place which in 1935 welcomed Britain's leading supporter of Adolf Hitler, Oswald Mosley – when he explained his 'facist policy' (how fabulous that whoever organised the posters couldn't actually spell fascist) to all the local would-be Nazis at a free meeting (should that read rally?) – was also home to a host of less dangerous events such as Christmas fayres, bingo (3s 6d (17p) to get in with the promise of a free pie), summer bazaars and flower, dog and bird shows – but obviously not all at the same time.

Chapter 6

BRIAN JONES HAD A GREEN BICYCLE

In March 1964, before I joined, the *Newsman* had launched a pop column of sorts called 'Round The Sound Track'. It was edited by Andrews junior and focussed on the plethora of local bands who were springing up like Japanese knotweed - Lee Scott and the Roulettes, Mark Shelley and the Deans, the Nite-Beats, Dean Austin and the Dominators and Ray Ford and the Statesmen plus a host more who all played around the local scene.

My huge fascination with pop music and all that went with it – there was the fame and the money not to mention the stories of sex, drugs and rock'n'roll – made the 'Sound Track' column a must for me and 1965 was my year for persuading Andrews the younger that I was the person to get stuck into, explore (and perhaps even expose) the British pop scene.

It all began in February when I went to see the great Chuck Berry at Southend Odeon and I told my new readers that "Saturday night's Chuck Berry show saw a preview of

the sound to come in the near future." After a glowing review of Berry and The Moody Blues, I moved on to bravely
predict that "a sound that may well catch the attention of
fans soon came along from Long John Baldry and The Graham Bond Organisation". Some prediction that turned out
to be as Baldry went on to have a grand total of two Top 20
singles and Bond just one Top 40 album!! But I had made
my point in print and boldly stood by it.

A month later I took the train (again) to Southend to interview The Rolling Stones who were on tour with The Hollies,
Dave Berry and Goldie and The Gingerbreads plus compere
Johnny Ball, the father of TV presenter Zoe, who worked as
a club and cabaret entertainer. It proved surprisingly easy
to get tickets for these shows and also to set up interviews
through the acts' management who seemed to agree that
all (even local) publicity was good publicity.

It was only years later, when I was working as a press
officer at record companies and representing major artists
who were less than keen on doing interviews with the local
press, particularly when there were national and music papers plus regional radio and TV stations in the offing, that I
realised how lucky we were. It was the sixties, I was there
and I do remember it. B30 Stones poster. jpg

A blonde and attractive Chelmsford High School girl
called Jackie was my date for The Stones concert and interview – getting a girl to go out with you when there was
the chance they might meet one of their pop idols made
the whole dating thing a lot easier. However the highlight
of her evening was not my scintillating company or even
meeting The Stones but involved Allan Clarke, singer with
The Hollies. He was wandering around backstage asking
if anyone had a comb. Quick as a flash I offered him my
rather grubby, mock turtle shell (plastic) multi-toothed ef-

fort which, when he'd finished, Jackie asked if she could
have as a memento. Over fifty years on she may still have
it in her box of treasured souvenirs; I know I had to buy
another comb.

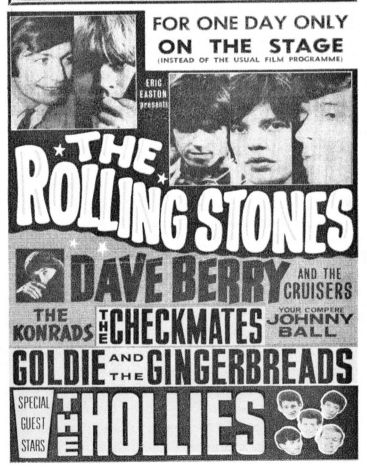

ABOVE: A collection of suited Hollies with the very well-groomed - thanks to a certain person's comb - Allan Clarke (right back row) alongside (front row l to r) Bobby Elliott and Eric Haydock and (back row l to r) Tony Hicks and Graham Nash.

LEFT: There they all were at Southend Odeon on March 17 1965 – the penultimate venue on the Rolling Stones' 14 night debut tour of the UK which began in London and ended in Romford with Liverpool, Sunderland, Leicester and Rochester in between.

Interviewing The Rolling Stones was something of a coup even if there were only four of them in their cramped dressing room backstage at the Southend Odeon. As we were about to get started Mick Jagger suddenly asked, "Where's Bill?" He was looking for Bill Wyman who had gone missing and like an embarrassed schoolboy I raised my hand and said that I had seen him disappearing behind the curtain at the back of the stage with a young lady – could have been a Gingerbread, who knew? Jagger rolled his eyes, explaining that the bass player had "probably gone for a 'knee trembler'" and added, "He's much better at that than this anyway."

So we got underway without Wyman (who did appear a bit later after his furtive rendezvous) and it all began with Jagger, who was hugging a large Gonk (a strange furry sixties toy with googly eyes) given to him by a fan, suggesting Southend fans weren't top of the pile when it came to showing their appreciation. "This isn't the best reception we have had but it was certainly a good one."

He then went on to explain where the band hung out in their time off. "We spend our leisure time in the Ad-Lib club when we can get there. Unfortunately we only manage that now and again." Then guitarist Keith Richard – this was the time when he had dropped the 's' from his surname on the advice of manager Andrew Loog Oldham as apparently it sounded "more rock n roll" – gave me an insight into the band's earnings.

He explained, "We don't know how much we earn each week or each year and being number one makes no difference financially. All our money is deposited so at the moment our earnings are as much a secret to us as to you." We may have shared a secret but I reckoned their savings were a lot more than mine although I did have a (just the one) Premium Bond.

While Charlie Watts said absolutely nothing throughout the half hour I spent with the group, Brian Jones showed himself to be an unnecessarily unpleasant young man who insisted on calling me a "c***" for some unknown reason and telling me about his bicycle. "I've got a bike, it's green with white mudguards and drop handlebars." As I left he added, "I've lost some spokes you know, somebody kicked them out."

With that I made my excuses and we got the train back to Chelmsford armed with my trusted notebook and a new insight on how drugs might impact on the brain but minus a comb. Despite my hopes of a fruitful finale to the evening with Jackie, I was also about to be minus a girlfriend as she had been quick to phone her mother from Southend station to arrange a pick up when we got to Chelmsford. She left me with nothing more than a thank you while I was left to walk the couple of miles home on a dark and chilly spring evening, all the time wondering whether getting to know The Stones made up for getting nowhere with Jackie.

And there was more disappointment to come when the paper came out on Tuesday. For this first-hand report of life with The Stones – which featured a set of the band's pre-signed autographs – I didn't even get a name check even though I managed to get the first person singular into the story at least once which must have left readers wondering who the 'I' was.

The same month saw Georgie Fame come to the Corn Exchange although I interviewed him before the show in the White Hart pub next door. Surprisingly nobody recognised him as he told me, "I do intensely dislike the colour bar. I find it intolerable and ridiculous." He also said that his fave (it was a hip word back then) drink was bourbon and his fave food was fou fou (semolina, spices & meat) which was a recipe given to him by his band's African drummer.

May 1965 saw the column carry the story of local bands Lee Scott and the Roulettes and the Nite-Beats competing against each other in the *Melody Maker* beat contest held in Wimbledon and judged by the audience. They voted the Nite-Beats into third place behind bands from East London and Ilfracombe and in his piece Rodney Andrews offered his opinion on the result, commenting; "For far too long they (Nite-Beats) have been underpaid (I know they will agree there) and grossly underrated."

In the same issue I made a memorable first personal appearance reviewing Bob Dylan's Albert Hall concert on May 9 which was at the end of his debut UK tour. I had gone to the show in London (remember it was 9s.6d for a cheap day return on the train) with Cummins who was a bit of a folkie at heart but for some reason I ended up giving my opinion of the up-and-coming 23 year-old American folk star as he played to an audience including assorted Beatles and Searchers – and was rewarded with a first ever in print credit … albeit a simple B.Southall.

Under the inspired headline 'Dylan Show', I wrote; "One man with just a guitar and a handful of harmonicas – a small man dressed in blue trousers and casual shirt and a leather jacket with a voice that seemed to fill the whole of the Albert Hall." It was obvious even back then that I recognised great talent when I saw it and went on to say; "On Sunday he showed what great talent he has and that not everybody needs a full orchestral backing or an electric guitar."

The man himself, who had topped the UK album charts for the first time a month earlier with *The Freewheelin' Bob Dylan* (the inspiration for my jacket, remember), was obviously so moved by what I wrote that within a month he had abandoned acoustic music and taken to appearing with an electric backing band. Good to know I played some small part in his career development although when I met him briefly many years later he didn't mention it.

In fact he didn't say anything at all. I bumped into him in the street in Mayfair in the mid-seventies when he was out shopping with his PR lady who was a friend of mine. We then had a ten minute supposedly three-way conversation – me, her and his Bob-ness – during which he said nothing, not a word, nada … but it was still a memorable moment.

May 1965 and Bob Dylan's Albert Hall concert gets the thumbs-up in the *Chelmsford Newsman* from the author, but the folk singer, who got second billing in the paper to news of a heat in the Melody Maker Beat contest held in Wimbledon, still went 'electric' soon after.

But it wasn't just Southend Odeon and the Corn Exchange that attracted the hit bands of the sixties to Essex.
For reasons unknown to me The Nashville Teens turned up
at Tufnell Hall in Little Waltham in August 1965. This was
a village where I would later play football – alongside future professionals Bryan King (Millwall and Coventry) and
Peter Collins (Tottenham Hotspur) – and we trained and
sweated and groaned in the very room where a crowd of
youngsters crammed in to see the band that made the hit
'Tobacco Road'.

Those fans, who paid 7s 6d. to get in, were disappointed
when the group turned up an hour late and played for just
30 minutes although they explained to me, and it appeared
a few days later in black and white so it must have been
true, that they had played another show earlier and got
delayed. They did go on to explain that the money they
made from doing two shows in one night wasn't important
to them … but I thought maybe it was to whoever did their
bookings.

The other band on the bill that night were an outfit from
Southend called Bubbles & Co – so-called because their
lead singer had a mass of blonde curls – and I did a brief interview with them for a short article for the pop page. They
were quite reasonably relegated to the away dressing room
and when we emerged after our chat there were a few girls
hanging around in the hall – and one of them was Jackie
from our night with The Stones.

She was with a girl friend and I introduced Bubbles (&Co)
to the girls, describing Jackie as my ex-girlfriend which
sounded sort of cool. I didn't mind admitting I had an 'ex' –
in fact I had a bunch 'exs' around town - and even though
they had all dropped me, I still thought it made me sound
like a lothario, a player, a Casanova if you will.

When Jackie invited us all back to her very family's impressive large detached house about ten miles away near Braintree, we all piled into the Bubbles band wagon and headed east. Once there, Jackie and I think Bubbles disappeared to some secret place, as did her friend with one of the Co while the rest of us played music, chatted, smoked and drank beer (them) and coke (me). Eventually it all came to an end and the band dropped me off in Chelmsford on their way back to Southend.

It was now close to six in the morning and I was excited about completing my first pop all-nighter but filled with foreboding about how it would go down with my parents, even though I was nearly eighteen and a wage earner who contributed to the housekeeping. I crept into the house, took off my boots and coat and took a seat in the front room to see how things played out. When my father came downstairs, I went with a story about getting in at around 1.30pm and, not wanting to wake anybody, had decided to sleep in an armchair.

I don't think for one minute he believed me and even if he did he still laid into me about staying out real late, not telling people where I was and added, just for good measure, that hanging around with long haired pop groups would get me nowhere. In actual fact hanging around with hirsute musicians turned out to be the making of me and led to a successful and profitable 40 year career in the music business but I had the good sense never to mention this to my father.

But it wasn't just modern music and musicians that my father didn't appreciate. He was predominantly a fan of all things sporting which he had written about for over 20 years and didn't go for very much in the way of light entertainment. On the other hand my mother was a big fan of films, musicals and singers like Frank Sinatra, Dean Martin and Dickie Valentine with even a little bit of Elvis or Cliff thrown in. Maybe my ending up as a writer and an aficionado of all things pop does mean it's all in the genes.

In the summer of 1965 my reporting skills were put to the test when I was in a van with a load of drunken, drug-fuelled rock musicians just as a real story lit up the horizon. I was leaving the nearby town of Witham where The Pretty Things – for it was them – had been playing in a local hall.

The five piece R&B band were working on the back of their only British top ten hit 'Don't Bring Me Down' and some lurid tales in the national newspapers about their behaviour. They were, a bit unfairly I always thought, considered to be a poor man's Rolling Stones while lead singer Phil May boasted that he was the man with the longest hair in Britain. None of that was important as the band offered me a lift back to Chelmsford – on their way to London – in their official van.

They were loud, rude and very funny until we came to a dead stop after less than a mile as a traffic jam built up and a glowing blaze lit the night sky. Then a policeman appeared next to the van, something which always put the fear of God into any law-breaking, drug- toting rock musician. But he was not there to search them or their van, merely to tell us that there was a large house fire ahead and all the roads were blocked to allow the fire brigade to do their work.

Immediately I put on my imaginary scribe's hat and told the boys in the band that I was off to get the scoop. They weren't overly impressed or the least bit helpful as they locked the doors and barred my way out of the van. Eventually they got bored, let me out and I made my way to where the action was, and told the police and fire brigade that I was a reporter – and I had an NUJ card to prove it.

Apparently the historic house Witham Lodge was on fire and fire engines had been called from far and wide to deal with the blaze. It seemed that the house wasn't occupied, but there was still a story to be filed and having got as much detail as I could, I went off in search of a phone box – which was what you did in the days before mobile phones.

As I dialled my editor Ken Andrews at home to give him the facts, I was given a raucous send-off by The Pretty Things as they finally made their way back to the capital. I passed on the facts to Andrews, who jotted them down and turned them into a story he would try and sell overnight to the nationals while also calling up one of the paper's photographers and urging him to get to Witham before the flames went out.

The time that passed between the weekend fire and publication of the *Newsman* on Tuesday gave me the chance to find out some more about the house, the fire and the damage it caused and add that to my on-the-spot reportage. I discovered that six fire engines from around the county were called and was able to report that they "fought the fire throughout the night" while adding that "by morning only a charred shell remained of the stately home."

The fact that my exclusive frontline coverage ended up wrapped into a piece about lightning strikes and fires throughout Essex over that same weekend was a disappointment, along with the fact that I didn't get a by-line --- after all I had risked my life (albeit from around 100yards away) to get the story.

In all honesty both the *Chronicle* and *Newsman* were very reluctant to hand out by-lines on stories. Odd features and various reviews might bring a name-check, but in the main news stories – even front page headline scoops – were published without a by-line. This was disappointing not just from an egotistical point of view (we all liked to see our names in print) but it also meant that you were never going to get noticed by the great journalistic talent spotters in Fleet Street – if there were any such people.

And to add insult to injury my interview with The Pretty Things from their Witham show appeared in the same edition (also without a credit) but with no mention of the fire down the road – probably a mistake on my part not to link the two. It did, however, include details of my misguided and overly generous offer to buy the band a round of drinks --- "double vodkas with coke and ice, whisky and coke and brandy and coke" was their order while I, being a teetotal, athletic Adonis, almost certainly stuck with orange juice. I do remember upsetting a surly barman by asking (nay insisting) on a receipt for my expenses claim.

Chapter 7

WHO'S REPORTING WHO?

I met The Who just before their show on December 4 1965 and for the first time understood and appreciated the appeal of a life in rock 'n' roll. They were using an area on the first floor of the Corn Exchange as a dressing room and when I arrived to interview them, I took in a scene that was totally new to me.

There were countless bottles of alcohol, boxes of pills laid out on top of instrument cases and maybe four or five attractive young ladies in mini-skirts and flimsy tops. Were they the groupies that I had read about who followed pop stars around offering 'favours' or were they their girl-friends, wives or even possibly sisters? Who knew but whatever they were they made an unforgettable impression on my innocent young eyes and set the blood racing through my veins.

Then, and this was the coup-de-grace, one of the group's managers – either Chris Stamp or Kit Lambert – turned up with a handsome leather case which he opened to reveal a selection of neatly packed one pound and five pound notes. This was the band's fee plus, and years later I came to understand how it worked, a share of the ticket receipts, and suddenly it all came together for me – rock music, girls, drink, drugs and loadsamoney. Even though I was incapable of playing any instrument, was teetotal and had only taken Aspro, I immediately thought what's not to like about a rock and roll lifestyle?

I spoke to both Roger Daltrey and Pete Townshend but it was the band's lead guitarist who gave me the exclusive story about The Who. Talking about rumours that the band had thoughts about breaking up, Townshend told me; "Yes, at one time we were contemplating a break-up. We were bored and we weren't getting the money. But we denied it to everyone." Now I was armed with a genuine exclusive story and it appeared in the December 7 1965 edition of the *Chelmsford Newsman* under the banner headline: 'The Who speak the truth!' with the sub heading: 'Bust Up Rumour Told To Newsman'.

And I was that newsman who came up with the exclusive but I all got in return was the same simple credit line of B.Southall - but this time in bold type - at the end of the article while Andrews had his photograph splashed under the title 'Round The Sound Track by Rodney Andrews'. And of course to cap it all, The Who never broke up and, even with two of their original line-up dead, they are still going over 50 years later. So much for me getting the pop scoop of the decade.

For reasons I still don't understand, 'Round The Sound Track' came to an end in March 1966, exactly two years after it first appeared. Maybe Andrews left the paper, maybe the paper decided pop was no longer a suitable subject, or maybe it was becoming more difficult to get records or interview bands. Either way it finished while the 'Saturday Scene' concerts went on until 1969, the same year as

B. Southall is at again with his *Chelmsford Newsman* scoop on The Who's possible break-up. The fact that they didn't split and are still going today despite the death of two original members took nothing away from the author's 'exclusive' story from December 1965

Chelmsford's Corn Exchange was demolished in an act of corporate vandalism.

Alongside the shows at the Corn Exchange, Chelmsford's thriving folk music scene held meetings and gigs in an upstairs room of the White Hart in Tindal Street. While I never actually interviewed any folk artists – most of the time I had no idea what they were going on about – I did pop along to sit among the beer swigging, pipe smoking beardies (probably with Lou Cummins who was all three) and caught Bert Jansch, Martin Carthy and the Singing Postman who, incidentally, was awful.

Back in the sixties I did my record buying at Daces in London Road where the pop department was up a single winding staircase which took you away from the more impressive instrument, sheet music and classical collections on the ground floor. Upstairs the albums (covers only) were arranged in bins in the middle of the room while singles were kept in racks behind the counter.

To the left of the counter, down a short flight of stairs, were four or five listening booths where us teenagers crammed in on a Saturday morning to play up to half a dozen singles or maybe a couple of albums which were given to us in just their inner bags. I and my mates spent hours in Daces listening to records and spent a good deal of our pocket money or hard earned wages buying the hits of the day and I have to admit that Daces was also the scene of a major heist in the summer of 1964.

The Rolling Stones first album – cunningly entitled *The Rolling Stones* so as not to confuse people – came out in May and as I had already bought both their singles 'Come On' and 'I Wanna Be Your Man', the album was a must have item for me. But at 32s/6d (£1.62p) it was a bit of a stretch for a poor schoolboy so, after listening to the album in the booth, I took a risk and placed the album - minus its glossy cover - down the back of my trousers under the cover of a thigh length raincoat.

Then, with a couple of pals acting as noisy distractions, it was a case of getting down the narrow twisty staircase and out of the front door without snapping the delicate vinyl disc in half. Shamefacedly I have to admit that I made it and still have the LP to this day – sans its bright shiny sleeve.

However if you didn't want to go to Daces, the Co-op in Moulsham Street, just a stone's throw from the High Street – the stone bridge over the River Can (before it merged with the River Chelmer) signified the end of one road and the beginning of the other – had a much more modern record department.

It had the latest listening booths on the wall which you stepped into after asking for a particular disc to be played. And the added attraction was Pat the girl who played the records; she was tall, blonde, dressed in a seductive, shiny, blue nylon Co-op uniform which rustled when she moved. And she was an older woman albeit by only about five years but she was still the stuff of teenage fantasies.

In the High Street you could also laze about in Lyons Tea House or pop across to Wainwrights Milk Bar on the corner of Tindal Street and London Road. This was genuinely a bar both in name and layout with stools at the counter and also at the single long table that faced the outside world. I had a girlfriend who worked there so I spent more time in there than was acceptable to the rather grumpy Mr Wainwright and once we broke up (me and her not me and Mr Wainwright) I swore never to darken his or its door – or drink his or its milkshakes - ever again. Can't remember whether I kept that promise as she left for college in London and I loved a milkshake.

Her going to college and eventually being swept off her feet by some flash student who apparently knew the fancy ways of London town's lunchtime sandwich haunts was a moment of heartbreak and teenage angst for me – and for more than just the obvious rejection I'd suffered.

I had taken her to see The Graham Bond Organisation at Southend Odeon when Bond, drummer Ginger Baker, bass player Jack Bruce and saxophonist Dick Heckstall-Smith were part of the package tour with The Moody Blues and Chuck Berry.

Bond was an overweight, sweaty man who sported long sideburns, an eccentric moustache and wore dark glasses even indoors and at night. I described him in my interview as looking every bit like "a refugee from Spain" even though I had never actually seen a refugee from Spain or anywhere else for that matter.

He played the organ with great gusto, and his talented quartet were my new fave raves but such was my anger at being dumped that when I went to the girl's house to retrieve my copy of the album *The Sound of 65*, I smashed it across my knee (you could do that with vinyl records) in order to make some point or other ... but I don't remember what exactly.

It took a long while to get over the disappointment of losing that record but eventually in the early 2000s I bought a copy of the album on CD (coupled with the group's follow up album *There's A Bond Between Us*) and once again all was well with the world.

The Orpheus remained my favourite hidey-hole but somewhere along the line in the summer of 1965 it was taken over by two ex-policemen called Rice and Bond who renamed it the R&B (clever stuff – Rice & Bond, rhythm and blues = R&B) and somehow they managed to put on local bands despite the place being no bigger than my mum's front room.

One of the new owners – described as a former wrestler – told me on the record, "We are quite determined not to have any trouble." Somehow he failed to mention the baseball bat that was kept under the counter to help keep the peace.

They were a couple of scary characters who were always happy to hand out a bit of ex-police brutality, however, somewhere along the line, it all went very wrong for the pair of them. One of them ran off with the other one's wife while that other one then teamed up with a strange (and much younger) early 'goth' girl before putting his police training to good use and becoming a criminal – but not quite a mastermind.

Meanwhile I did my time in local Rural District Council meetings, which involved themselves with the business of the villages around Chelmsford from Boreham to Stock and Margaretting to Pleshey. They weren't the source of great news exclusives, although the moment a local councillor for Danbury spoke up against the condoms which were being strewn about the local common made for a few good lines. He said something very quotable about condoms "hanging from bushes like Christmas fairy lights."

The local Hospital Management Committee meetings were a tad more enjoyable (or less boring) although I gradually came to realise that none of these meetings were supposed to be fun. Here they discussed bed pans, car parking, nurse's uniforms and what colour to paint the wards. However, on occasions financial reports were produced and discussed and that gave us something to get our teeth into especially when they showed that things in the NHS were financially challenged even back then.

In my early teens my knowledge of medical practices was pretty much limited to irregular visits to the doctor – no appointments necessary, you just turned up, sat in the waiting area and waited your turn – until a fateful day in May 1960 when the nation celebrated the wedding of Princess Mar-

garet to Anthony Armstrong-Jones. It was a Friday and we
all had a day off school but rather than watch a stuffy old
wedding on the telly – it was the first royal wedding to be
broadcast live – my brother and I opted to play football in
Oaklands Park.

It was there, as I emulated the skills of my hero, Aston
Villa, and future England, centre forward Gerry Hitchens,
that I broke a bone in my foot. It required a trip to hospital
for an x-ray and a bit of bandage – apparently broken
metatarsal bones did not need plaster – a few aspirins and
plenty of rest but alas no football for a few weeks.

The fact that Hitchens – a real live professional footballer
- was a friend of the family (my family!) was proper 'Roy of
the Rovers' stuff for a soccer crazy kid like me. The former
coal miner had been helped on his way to a career that
spanned Cardiff, Aston Villa, AC Milan and England by my
father who reported on his games for Kidderminster Har-
riers and mentioned him to a football scout he knew which
kicked off the whole thing as he was transferred to the capital city of Wales for the princely sum of £1500.

Whenever he and Cardiff or Villa played in London,
Hitchens made sure we got tickets for his games and we
always met up afterwards for a chat. He was a genuine First
Division player who knew me and called me Brian ... it was
the stuff of dreams. I took advantage of this relationship to
arrange an interview with Gerry (that's what I called him)
during my brief stint on *Goal* magazine in 1970 and we
stayed in touch until his untimely death aged 48 in 1983
after he collapsed during a charity football match.

But the highlight of our friendship had come in 1961
when Hitchens played for England on an end of season
tour to Portugal, Italy and Austria and sent the Southalls
a postcard from Rome (where he scored two goals in a 3-2

victory over Italy) plus a photograph of the entire England squad, signed by all the players. A keepsake that is kept safe to this day.

On May 24 1961, the very day he scored two goals for England against Italy in Rome, centre forward Gerry Hitchens sent my father a fancy coloured postcard from Rome

Going to see Aston Villa was something my brother (even though he was a Wolves fan) and I did with my father and it almost always involved a local derby on Boxing Day. We spent most Christmases with my grandparents in Worcestershire and after the Christmas Day festivities

would make our way – usually in my uncle Joe's car - to either Villa Park, Molineux, St Andrews or the Hawthorns to see a blood thirsty encounter between the best the Midlands could offer.

> Gerry Hitchins also sent over in a separate envelope
> a postcard of the England squad for their games in
> Portugal, Italy and Austria. It was signed by 18 of the
> players pictured (plus manager Walter Winterbottom)
> and among the squad is one future England manager,
> two record goal scorers, Britain's first £100 a week foot-
> baller and at least six club captains

Villa Park was the venue for the 1963 Christmas game against local rivals Wolves (described in the programme as "valued friends and foe") which ended all square at 2-2 with Harry Burrows scoring twice for Villa and Chris Crowe and Ray Crawford replying for the visitors. The centre of the programme - between the two team line-ups – featured an advert telling you that "Senior Service Satisfy." There was no such thing as a non-smoking dressing room back then.

I pretty much concentrated on football injuries back then – sprained ankles, split lips and, once, excitingly, water on the knee – but things took a turn for the worse in December 1965 as everybody prepared for Christmas. My paternal grandfather died aged 75 and we all trooped up to Stourport-on-Severn for his funeral. For reasons I still don't really understand his body was still in his house when we got there and for the first time in my life I found myself looking at a dead body.

I don't know what I expected but the old feller didn't look well. He was shrunken and sort of waxy – and without his regulation trilby - and while nobody ever told me what he died of, it was probably cancer but that was a disease that was never mentioned back then. Whatever the cause, it probably wasn't helped by his regular diet of bread and dripping, pints of ale, unfiltered Woodbines and drinking his tea from a saucer rather than a cup. What was it with old people and pouring tea from a cup into a saucer so they could blow on it?

Chapter 8

I FOUGHT THE LAW AND...

Back at work I was spending a lot of time sitting in courts of various levels – magistrates, quarter sessions and assizes – and over time became quite fascinated by the law. So fascinated in fact that I toyed with the idea of quitting life as a journalist to take up life as a solicitor or, even better, a barrister before ending up, naturally, as a High Court judge.

Watching and listening to the arguments and excuses that spilled forth from the be-wigged gentlemen of the bar was an education and even more attractive was the idea of being in charge and actually doling out the sentences. What power! That was until a solicitor's clerk explained what you had to go through just to get where he was on the greasy pole that led to the bench.

Apparently there were books (hundreds of them) to be read and exams (quite a few of them too) to be taken before they let you anywhere near a courtroom. And you couldn't just start out by doing the tasty criminal stuff, you had to study civil, maritime, corporate, international, tax and a whole bunch more 'laws' before you got the chance to deal with gangland thugs like the Kray brothers, traitors such as Soviet spy George Blake, drug-taking Rolling Stones or even a Sainsbury's shoplifter.

So with all that information I opted for reporting the cases and it turned out to be educational, often eye-opening and occasionally quite a lot of fun but not always for the guys and gals in the dock.

I began by covering Chelmsford's magistrates courts which sat regularly three times a week – Monday, Wednesday and Thursday - but they would throw in an odd Friday or even Saturday morning session if the police nabbed a serious offender who they wanted to keep in custody.

These courts, and often there was more than one, took place in the Shire Hall, the town's centre piece at the top of the High Street which was opened as the "dispenser of justice" in 1791, and still stands (although sadly unused) next to a statue of Judge Tindal, a distinguished lawyer and MP who was born in Chelmsford and died in 1846.

He was educated at the town's King Edward VI grammar school and in 1820 successfully defended the UK's Queen Consort, Caroline of Brunswick, wife of King George VI, when she was tried for adultery. In later years his statue became the butt of a few college 'rag day' pranks and he was often seen sporting a variety of fancy hats and even a few traffic cones. Not the most dignified look for such a distinguished local KEGS lad who made good.

On the days when the magistrates were in session on the first or second floors of the ornate cavernous building, the regular practice was for some of the accused - not the proper villains who were kept locked up across the road in the police station until it was time for their day in court - their families, witnesses, solicitors, us reporters and the police to hang around on the stairs. When the magistrates, together with the clerk to the court arrived, we were allowed in but that didn't always go smoothly.

The police had a strange sense of humour which came with the authority they could wield coupled with the fact that back then there was not a lot you could do if you wanted to keep on the right side of the law in the quest for info. Their idea of a joke was not to everyone's taste but no matter, it was their gag or jape and everybody else had better find it funny. There was no arguing with a bobby when it came to a practical joke.

I was the victim of one of their jolly pranks and it was one that wasn't even half funny as it could have cost me my job. When the magistrates courts opened for business and we all began to make our way up the stairs, it was a shock to find that I had been, during what I thought was a friendly tête à tête with the detectives, secretly handcuffed to the stair rail and was unable to get to work. And no amount of pleading would persuade them to release me.

Leaving me out there, cuffed and being stared at like a dangerous villain, was, in their minds, hilarious and me being left stranded for anything up to three hours – the morning court session ran from 10am until 1pm – and unable to cover any cases and file any copy was of no importance to the boys in blue (plain clothes actually) who eventually released me when they tired of the joke or had to go back to the station.

With a bit of luck and a fair wind I might have got a helping hand that day with some copy from one of the other reporters who was 'free' to go to work but it was touch and go and meant that the favour would have to be returned one day. However, if it had all gone wrong and there was no copy sharing, then I would have been left to explain to the hierarchy of Ken Andrews, Josie Spargo or Stuart Birch just what had happened. And when I did tell them they thought it was sort of funny but the best advice I got was to keep my hands in my pockets at all times whenever I was near a policeman. Not very helpful but better than getting the sack and a motto I've lived by ever since.

It didn't end there with the police and their merry ways. One Christmas Eve, after making the regular call to the front desk to catch up on events, I was unceremoniously grabbed by the DCs and frog-marched to the cells in Chelmsford's police station. And there I stayed until the afternoon when they decided the joke was over or more likely it was their going home time. I don't think I even got a cup of tea but it did give me my one and only insider's view of a 1960s police cell and I can confirm that, in December, they are not very comfortable and are bloody cold.

The same two detectives – I remember their names even now, nearly sixty years on, and could easily pick them out in a line-up – also thought that driving an unmarked police car on to the pavement in the High Street, jumping out, grabbing me and putting me up against the wall to 'pat me down' for weapons before handcuffing me and bundling me into the car was fun. It was all too early for The Sweeney but it had definite overtones of *Fabian of the Yard* or Inspector Lockhart in *No Hiding Place* rather than *Dixon of Dock Green*.

This was marginally better than being left in a cell for four hours but it did give my mum a scare as a woman who recognised me, telephoned her to say that I had been arrested and taken away in handcuffs. It seems that my mother then made a call to my father who checked it out with his reporter colleagues who in turn spoke to the police and eventually worked out that it was all just a joke, a jolly jape, a little bit of harmless fun.

As a tee-total teenager I didn't socialise with the members of the constabulary who in the main were hard and regular drinkers, but my new girlfriend Pat (later to become my wife – she was the one who didn't dump me) and I were invited to a party at the house of a Welsh copper called – wait for it – Taffy. To this day I don't know quite why we were asked along but it was a harmless night during which I learned that Taffy had become a policeman despite having been arrested in Wales for being drunk in charge of a bicycle.

He was also one of the coppers who if they saw me cycling home – with or without lights – would stop the patrol car, bundle my bike into the boot or on to the back seat and drop me off at home. On occasions the journey would involve a trip to the local soft drinks and crisps depot in New Street where, courtesy of helpful but mis-named security men, cases of pop and cartons of snacks destined for the nick, would join me and my bike in the car. Spoils of war I think they called it.

Bicycles were very much the machine for us teenagers in the sixties while cars were reserved for grown-ups, mods went for scooters and rockers favoured a bigger motor bike. And back then push bikes were ridden properly – with the all-important pair of bicycle clips - on the road along with cars and buses.

There was none of this riding on the pavement or the wrong way up a one way street or going across a red traffic light because you can. For reasons I don't recall, I don't think I ever used my bike to travel to the office or to go off to court hearings or meetings – there was something demeaning about turning up on a green bike with red handlebar grips and padlocking it to the railings outside the Shire Hall. Not very Bob Woodward or Carl Bernstein

Young love – Pat and me looking
suitably trendy in the sixties.
It all began in 1967 and we're still
reelin' in the years!

The laws for cyclists were strictly enforced by the police on foot patrol and in any given week, at least a third of the cases we saw brought before the magistrates involved cyclists having no lights, cycling on the pavement and even, in some extreme cases, having no brakes. They all resulted in small fines and to be fair we never bothered to report them as they were considered small fry when set alongside a spot of shoplifting or a careless driving case or a good old fashioned punch up.

When I did miss out on a juicy court case for whatever reason – maybe because I was cuffed to a stair rail - it often brought extra disappointment for editor Andrews as he also ran his own news agency on the side. I was never sure of the legal or ethical rights and wrongs of this business but it allowed him to take the court stories that I and my colleagues filed, and send truncated versions to the then popular London evening papers.

Chelmsford was in the heart of the commuter belt and the *Evening Standard* and *Evening News* were both staple reading for workers as they travelled home on the train or bought one of them at railway stations in Southend, Shenfield, Brentwood or Chelmsford.

With most of the defendants in our courts being local, it was always good to get the lowdown on who had done what and where and with whom before assembling it for the London papers. These short stories were known as 'news in brief' or NIBS and on more than one occasion I would end up calling the copy desk of the London papers from the *Chronicle's* Duke Street office to give them a NIB, using Ken Andrews like a spy codename to get through on a reverse charge call.

This meant that I gave copy I was paid to write for the *Chronicle* (or *Newsman*) to other newspapers, used a *Chron-*

icle phone to do so and saw Andrews pocket the money that was paid into his agency account. But as a young budding news hound who was still learning his trade and anxious to please, there were no complaints from me. I looked on it as a double blessing – I gained valuable experience and I didn't piss off my boss.

However there was a genuine sense of satisfaction coupled with a little bit of pride in seeing even the briefest four or five line story in the stop press column of the Standard or News. If I had filed something I would make a point of picking up a paper from the newsstands at Chelmsford station where a small, gnarled, always slightly inebriated paper seller known as Tiger held court and shouted "read all abaht it" at passing commuters.

What appeared was never more than a few lines but they were all mine even if they just read (always in bold type): "Chelmsford man Billy Goat (aged 23) was sent to prison for six months for rustling cattle with intent to make beef burgers." That was it; I was in a major London paper even if I wasn't credited – or paid.

But as time went by I got to know new things about my editor and not all of them were impressive. In 1964 I was playing football for the local Rainsford Youth Centre and near the end of that year's football season – around April, May time – we went off to Germany on an exchange trip which included three football matches.

We were based in a place called Wesel in the north of Germany which, during WWII had been 97% destroyed by Allied bombs and its population reduced from 25,000 before the war to just 1,900 by 1945. Nevertheless we were welcomed warmly during our stay with local families and went on trips to churches, museums and a chocolate factory.

A year later, by which time I was working at the *Chronicle* and no longer a youth or playing for Rainsford, the exchange part of the trip took place and the German boy I had stayed with came to my house for a fortnight. I didn't play in any of the return soccer games but did suggest our visitors took a trip around the *Essex Chronicle* to see how a newspaper was put together and printed

However when I mentioned it to Andrews and asked if it was OK for this group of German teenagers, none of whom had been born by the time the war ended, to visit, he was less than enthusiastic. In fact, had the owner R.A.F. Handley not agreed, he would have done his best to stop the whole thing for reasons that slowly became clear to me. He hated Germans, not just the ones he might have fought against, but all of them including the children who had nothing to do with the conflict and whose families had seen their own town and its people almost wiped out.

This was in total contradiction to my own father's attitude. He served on a Royal Navy mine sweeper during the war but bore no malice towards his former enemy and welcomed the young German lad who stayed with us into his home. He was also a friend (and a fan) of the German footballer and former WWII prisoner of war Alec Eisenträger who joined Chelmsford City in 1959.

The trip went ahead – and was featured in the paper with a story under the heading "Germans students see the works" - but Ken Andrews, like many a journalist before him, made his excuses and left. In fact he didn't make much of an excuse but just said that if Germans were coming into the building he wasn't going to be there. It was my first experience of genuine racism and hatred and it left me both flabbergasted and disappointed although it did convince me that a 1964 headline about four German police offices arriving in the town as guests of the Essex Constabulary probably came from the editor's pen. It read "Achtung! Polizei."

If being handcuffed to the court railings was an embarrassment and inconvenience, I had to put up with some more genuinely humourous if slightly worrying episodes during my time in the magistrates courts. I was once 'identified' by a witness when she was asked if there was anyone in the court who she saw commit the crime. If that wasn't bad enough I was also picked on while innocently sitting at the press bench, pen in hand, by a magistrate who mistook me for the guilty party and gave me a hefty fine for doing something illegal.

One of the worst culprits for magistrates' blunders was the tall, bespectacled Captain Wenley whose family were partners in the town's Bolingbroke and Wenley department store. He sat in the court pretty regularly but, it always seemed to me, failed to grasp the first essential rules for the job; identify the accused and work out the sentencing options before opening your mouth.

More than once, having removed his extra strong glasses, he peered around the court until his blurred gaze rested on someone, anyone, who looked the least bit dodgy. He would then stare at them and in his gravest tone send them to prison or fine them an outrageously hefty sum for the most petty of crimes until the clerk of the court, the enormously rotund Mr James or his equally large deputy 'Nobby' Clarke, stood and turned to whisper in the Captain's ear.

Then, armed with the details on the limits of any sentences he could impose, he would back-track and offer the offender the warning, "This time you will pay of a fine of £5 but next time it'll be prison for you, young man."

Even though I was covering the magistrates' courts on a

pretty regular basis I didn't know how you became a magistrate – what did you have to know (certainly not the law!) or perhaps more importantly, who did you have to know. The regulars in Chelmsford were, as far I could understand, among the great and good of the town – Messrs Raven (chair of the Rural District Council), Chapman (owner of a long standing High Street jewellers) Bellamy (chemist and future town Mayor), Captain Wenley and the former Mayors Ron Wicks and Jean Roberts.

There was no shortage of seemingly well intentioned local people who happily sat in the courts during the mid-sixties for no financial reward but maybe a good deal of local kudos. The rules said you had to have at least two and usually three magistrates for a hearing to take place with one being trained as a chairperson, and by the nineties the people in charge of these things had listed the following necessary requirements to serve as a magistrate. They were "good character", "maturity and sound temperament", "social awareness" and "sound judgement" – and it's likely that they weren't much different back in my day.

Standing as a magistrate and dispensing justice for the good and protection of the community had its drawbacks; the people you convicted and sentenced were never best pleased and often resorted to shouting obscenities and making wild and often violent threats. It was all usually shrugged off by the 'beaks' but they were put on high alert after one unsavoury incident in the local Central Park.

It involved a regular magistrate and well known businessman who was pounced on in the park after dark and attacked with a six inch nail stuck through a piece of wood. He was badly injured but survived and stoically continued with his duties. His attacker was never caught despite both the police and the press (and a lot of local ne'er-do-wells) knowing exactly who had done it but alas there were no witnesses and no proof. The culprit was a local career villain who the magistrate had sent down and someone I had known from school days but I had no evidence so there was nothing I could do about it.

Chapter 9

CHRISTMAS WITH SEBAG AND MELFORD

On occasions covering the courts also brought me some unwanted confrontations. The father of a boy I was at school with and regularly played football with, came round to my parents' house one evening to make me an offer he thought I couldn't refuse. If I was prepared not to report his son's case for assault (on a policeman I think) he would give me twenty quid … more than two weeks' wages.

While I never thought there was any underlying threat of violence towards me, just a father's desperate plea for me to help his son keep his job, I did go back indoors to get my father's advice on how to deal with the problem. Right from the outset I wanted to say 'no' as I knew accepting a bribe was wrong, both legally and morally, and I also realised that it would put me in a difficult position further down the line.

What I was concerned with was how to say no without appearing hard-hearted and unsympathetic; confrontation on this scale was not something I had ever faced before.

I was comfortable dealing with a short-sighted, illegitim-
ate referee or an irate striker I might have up-ended but
this was serious stuff that would impact on a family. In the
end my father came out and pointed out to the other father
that what he was asking me to do was wrong, that it was all
the fault of his own son as he had punched the other bloke
(or copper) and should take responsibility for what he had
done.

That settled it but of course, thinking back, there could
have been a Plan B. As it turned out I wasn't in the court to
cover this particular case so bribing me would have been
a pointless exercise but, as the father (wrongly) assumed I
had the authority to halt or pull any story, I could have just
taken to money, denied all knowledge of the meeting and
waited for a desperate dad to own up to attempting to bribe
me, a professional journalist.

While I got out of that potential problem unscathed there
were moments when it didn't go quite so smoothly. Some of
the people who appeared in the dock for sentencing were
on occasions given a tongue lashing by the magistrate and
then, for some reason, took exception to the report of their
case which appeared in the paper, often under a sensa-
tional headline.

It was usually the banner headings that upset them as
they were bigger and bolder and displayed prominently on
the page for all to see. And when the opportunity arrived to
use a good quote from the presiding magistrate in the story
it often included phrases such as; "menace to society", "violent thug", "stupid bully" or "mindless idiot."

What none of these rogues and villains realised was that
the bloke they saw in court was not the same person who
wrote the headlines; that was the sub editor's job and they
were people who remained invisible most of the time. I

tried to explain this to one young man who took exception to my report of his court appearance and told me so when he confronted me one evening as I walked along Victoria Road.

He was with his girlfriend and I was with a mate but that didn't stop him as he stood in front of me, called me a lot of nasty names and then, despite me suggesting the headline was "nothing to do with me guv", set about punching me. His girlfriend screamed for him to stop while my mate threw some strong words at him, none of which made any difference. He was now kicking me as I lay curled up in the street but, fortunately, after a few minutes he got bored and gave up.

Luckily I was wearing a black PVC raincoat, the sort which absorbed nothing and just dripped rainwater on to your thigh but fortunately it did soak up the impact of most of the kicks. I survived only slightly bruised and a bit battered but with my looks, if not my dignity, intact. There was no lasting damage but it was two lessons learned – always beat a hasty retreat if I recognised anyone from a court case I had covered and make sure to go out with mates who were handy with their fists.

There were half a dozen well-known thugs around Chelmsford who were always on the look-out for a punch-up and, fortunately, most of them didn't mind a bit of publicity – it only added to their reputation as hard men. One on-going feud between three of them and a well-known bouncer nicknamed 'Rubber', for obvious reasons, made for a few stories as they seemed to beat each other up with amazing regularity over a period of a few months.

There were, however, less violent criminals who were happy just to steal stuff, although one in particular displayed a surprisingly reasonable attitude towards his potential victims. Vicky was the best cat burglar in town – we all knew it even though we could never work out how a bloke who was around five foot six inches tall and a bulky 14 stone (that's 88.9 kgms or 196 lbs if you prefer) could manage to get through the smallest kitchen windows. But he did and very successfully for some years. He never resorted to violence, always left the scene of crime if there was any danger of him being caught in the act and showed unexpected respect for a mate one day when we chatted in the R&B.

I was with my friend Stuart (he was also Lee Scott of Roulettes fame) as we talked with Vic, and Stu happened to mention that his family lived in Springfield Road. "Which house?" asked Vic. "The big white one up near the end of the road not far from the Oasis café", said Stuart. Showing no emotion Vic casually remarked, "Good job you told me, I was thinking of doing some of them houses but I'll leave yours now I know." I was then tempted to tell Vic exactly where I lived in the hope that my home might also get knocked off his list of 'to do' gaffs.

One of the saddest scenarios I came across involved Bobby Hurst, younger brother of England World Cup hero Geoff. They both grew up in Chelmsford and my brother played in the same youth centre football team as Bobby who, like his big brother, was a formidable striker. However, I came across him in the courts in 1965 where Bobby appeared on a few occasions.

There was an assault charge, when he was described, harshly I thought, by the magistrate as "a curse to everybody", and a housebreaking offence when he was arrested IN the river by two policemen who went in after him as he tried to get away. At a special court hearing, following his attempted watery escape, we reported that Hurst appeared wearing a "pair of borrowed police trousers and no socks." However, nobody on the bench showed any sympathy for his situation and they sent him off to Borstal anyway.

In fact he was an amiable enough lad who tried hard to deal with his situation of living in the shadow of his famous brother – some suggested he was unfairly pushed down the family pecking order as Geoff's sporting status grew. I remember meeting him in the street one day and asking what he was up to. "I'm into coin collecting", he said before adding, with a grin, "Mainly other peoples." Sadly within ten years of his brother helping England lift the Jules Rimet trophy, Bobby committed suicide by jumping under a train at Chelmsford station.

Bobby Hurst wasn't the only person I knew who came before the court in the mid-sixties. There was another Bobby, who was in the same church choir as my brother and me, and he and his mate Bernie (it sounded like a comedy double act – the Bobby and Bernie show) were 'caught in the act' on the roof of the Odeon cinema trying to steal lead. They were done for possessing housebreaking implements and I remember thinking that whatever you had with you when you were clambering about on a roof in the middle of the night could be construed as a 'housebreaking implement'. They were both sent to prison and thankfully bore me no malice for the coverage they received in the paper. They might have reasoned it was their choice and my job.

When, in February 1965, the *Newsman* carried the headline "Coloured man on Wounding Charge", the story was accompanied by a photo of the man being led from the police station to court. Of course we would not have written "White man on wounding charge" but it was a different and not necessarily better time. It was also one of the unwritten laws of the police/press relationship that we always got a tip from them to tell us when an 'important/notorious' (read 'newsworthy') prisoner was being escorted across the road to court so we could dispatch a photographer to capture the moment.

Of course the police could have used the underground passage between the cells and the court room but it did the constabulary's image no harm for them to be seen escorting dangerous criminals across the road in handcuffs, while the good citizens of Chelmsford looked on safe in the knowledge that all was well with the world.

Promotion from the magistrates court took me into the Essex Quarter Sessions, which sat four times a year (quarterly, geddit?) in the same Shire Hall but on the ground floor in the custom-built courts which had docks, judges' benches, jury seats, a press box, public gallery and, of course, the tunnel leading from the cells in the nearby police station to the court.

Most of the court hearings were held under the watchful eye (and ear) of the chairman

J Roland Adams QC who handily lived not far away from Chelmsford in Great Leighs and was never late and expected everybody else - prisoners, lawyers, detectives, jurors and reporters to be just as punctual. He was a bit of a tyrant who handed out some pretty stiff sentences and gave me my first in-court telling-off when I tried to leave the press box during his sentencing in an effort to get ahead of the game.

My plan was to leave my seat, creep to the exit and hang around there eavesdropping until he finished his sentencing speech and then I would be first in line for one of the two telephones in the Hall's foyer. Unfortunately Adams was in full flow and took my efforts to get away from his thunderous dispensing of justice as a personal insult. As I took my first few tentative steps towards the door I heard a booming voice from behind me say something along the lines of, "Where do you think you're going? This is my court and you will not leave while I am speaking. Sit back down." So I did and then, just to add further to my punishment, I had to queue behind my rival writers to get to the phones.

The usual press team for the serious courts came from the *Chronicle, Essex Weekly News, East Anglian Daily Press,* based in Ipswich, the *Southend Standard* and the *Essex County Standard* from Colchester. There wasn't a regular court correspondent for either the *Chronicle* or *Weekly News* – both papers were in Chelmsford and could simply send along any reporter who was around although I did get the gig most days.

The other three regulars were a lot older than me – the two blokes, who were even older than my father and he was over forty, were always Mr Rouse (Southend) and Mr Vosper (East Anglia). The third member was a woman – an older woman but in that enticing way I had read about in dodgy books. She was attractive, brunette, charming and gave a young man the 'come on' without even trying or knowing. However all my lustful thoughts disappeared when she mentioned that her husband was copper; that was enough to scare me back to my senses and to girls of my own age.

After the Quarter Sessions, the Essex Assizes were the most senior courts and they dealt with the most serious cases which saw some of the top legal brains descend on Chelmsford - and when the judges came to town it was pomp and ceremony in equal measures.

The High Court judges, be-wigged and in bright red robes, walked from the nearby Cathedral, after a pre-court ser-vice, at the head of a parade which included the High Sheriff of the county, the town's Bishop, the Chief Constable of Essex and the Mayor of Chelmsford.

On occasions there were also purple-clad Circuit Judges who literally sat on the bench as subs for their High Court superiors. The procession, which stopped the traffic, featured people in frock coats, feathered hats, ruffed shirts, chunky chains, black stockings and buckled shoes and looked like a very early Gay Pride march but without the music.

The Essex Assizes attracted the great and good of the legal profession and during my many hours spent in the press box I witnessed amongst others Quintin Hogg, then a member of the Conservative Government, appear in a case although I can't remember which one. I know I looked on a bit starry-eyed as he was famous and I'd seen him on the telly and in the papers - and here he was in Chelmsford. Also appearing on the bill at the Essex Assizes during my time as a court reporter were a selection of the most powerful and important judges in the land.

Justice Frederick Lawton – who was referred to by everyone in the law community as 'Piggy' – was a former fascist who sent gang leader Charles Richardson to prison for 25 years in 1967, but a decade earlier had defended Russian Olympic discus thrower Nina Ponomareva on a charge of shoplifting from C&A in London's Oxford Street. It was a major diplomatic incident at the time and, after absconding for weeks, she eventually turned up, was found guilty and fined the princely sum of 3guineas (£3.15p OR roughly 310 Russian roubles).

From what I saw at first hand Lawton was a stern man who had no time for career criminals and he handed out the severest sentences at the drop of a wig and also courted controversy with helpful observations such as, "Wife beating may be socially acceptable in Sheffield, but it is a different matter in Cheltenham."

Another judge who regularly sat in Chelmsford was a man with one of the most memorable of first names - he was Justice Christmas Humphreys who way back in the 1920s was the UK's leading Buddhist. As a barrister he prosecuted Christopher Craig and Derek Bentley who were found guilty of murdering a policeman in 1952, Ruth Ellis who was convicted of murdering her lover in 1955 and Timothy Evans who was controversially found guilty of murdering his daughter in 1950. While Craig, who was just 16, was reprieved, the other three were all hanged, although Evans was declared innocent and granted a Royal Pardon in 1966.

The man who defended Ruth Ellis, who was the last woman to hang in Britain, was Justice Melford Stevenson who I saw regularly on the bench at Chelmsford during the 1960s and he was also prone to making the occasional odd remark to defendants. He once told a man acquitted of rape, "I see you come from Slough. It is a terrible place. You can go back there." In a similar vein he told a husband involved in a divorce case that his decision to live in Manchester was "a wholly incomprehensible choice for any free man to make".

He was not quite so "witty" when it came to dealing with the notorious Kray twins at their trial for murder in 1969. Sentencing Reggie and Ronnie to a minimum of 30 years inside, he explained, "In my view, society has earned a rest from your activities."

Thinking back there were some quite wonderful forenames (or Christian names as we happily called them). Alongside Christmas, Quintin and Melford there was also Sebag Shaw although we were still a long way from having judges called Wayne, Jason or Kylie and that was still the

case in 2020 when not one of the 104 High Court Judges
was called by any of those names but there is a Karen and
a Nat.

It has to be said that during my time in the Essex Assize
court, which was spent mostly in sombre reverence as
people's lives were either rescued or destroyed, there were
very few moments when we had a laugh. No matter that
some of it looked a bit ridiculous, it was not a music hall
and the players, sadly, were not entertainers there to be ap-
plauded or booed. It was serious stuff but just occasionally
there were moments when it was hard to keep a straight
face.

There was an Irishman called Foiker charged with stealing cigarettes from the Carreras depot at Basildon. It was
a major crime involving thousands of pounds worth of
fags but throughout the trial, the judge insisted on calling
the defendant – in his best public school voice – "Fucker".
When the poor man in the dock muttered apologetically
that it was pronounced "Foiker", his lordship told him in
no certain terms "You Fucker will keep quiet and not inter-
rupt me again." Needless to say, after being found guilty, Mr
Foiker was detained at her Majesty's Pleasure and I think
the trial ended with the judge telling him in no uncertain
terms, "You Fucker will go to prison for (can't remember
the exact number but it was quite a few) years. Take him
down."

We in the press box, along with the court ushers, the jury
and even some members of the legal teams, did our best
not to laugh out loud while some in the public gallery - obviously not Foiker's family - simply guffawed. The question
was did the judge, whose stony expression gave nothing
away, do it deliberately as his own little joke or was it
simply his rather posh way of pronouncing the defendant's

name? In the press box the smart money was on it being the judge's accent but we lived in hope that it was a bit of legal whimsy.

The job of the defence counsel required them on occasions to come up with some fanciful tales to try and get their client off. A legal argument was one thing, a case of mistaken identity another, while passing the blame to a co-defendant was not uncommon but the best of defences were often the most ridiculous and, it has to be said, entertaining.

When the dishevelled son of a traveller's family appeared charged with rape, there was no argument about the basic facts. The bloke was with a girl in his car parked in a field in the Essex countryside. They were, so to speak, getting it on when at some point she tried to put a stop to proceedings but, according to the prosecution, the lad continued and raped the girl.

One of the witnesses was a television script writer who was walking his dog in the same darkened field and his evidence was that he heard a male voice say, "Alright then give us a wank." The defence counsel, arguing that the girl was a willing and consensual partner and was not raped, then came up with a line that sent the court into fits of stifled laughter. He suggested to the middle aged, respectable dog walker that what he in fact heard was his client saying, "Alright then give us a crank" as the car had broken down and wouldn't start.

Unsurprisingly it didn't wash with the jury and the young man was convicted and sent to prison and all that was left for us to do, when we gathered in the press room later, was to imagine how long the defence barrister had spent thinking up words which rhymed with "wank". Could he have come up with, "Alright I'll go to the bank" and suggested that his client might at some time have to go get some cash or perhaps "Alright I'll go get a plank" if the car was stuck in the muddy field.

It was ingenious and exactly what this particular legal brain was being paid to do – come up with a line that would get the youngster off but it sounded so ridiculous and implausible that it, perhaps, sealed his fate with the jury who were not about to be taken for fools and subsequently found him guilty.

The courts were a hive of activity but occasionally there was a genuine light-hearted moment that relieved the hours of keeping your head down and your pen poised. One afternoon a bloke who was hanging around waiting to see how his mate in the dock got on, decided to come and sit in the room that we reporters commandeered as our haven between cases. I think it was intended as the cloakroom where witnesses, policemen and women plus assorted hangers-on could leave their coats while they were off doing important court stuff.

While he was waiting, the chap came and sat with us and in his Cockney twang started chatting harmlessly about things of no consequence or interest. Then he pulled out a pack of cards and invited us to 'find the lady', but he had the good sense not to ask us to put our money where our mouths were. When we had all failed miserably to work out which card was the Queen as he swiftly moved them around the table, he pulled out three walnut shells and pea and we began a session of the 'shell game'; and once again we were rubbish at finding the pea under the shell as he pushed them here and there while keeping-up a never-ending stream of patter.

But it was a fun way to while away the time we had during a court recess for legal arguments or while the jury pondered their decision. The good news for him was that no coppers turned up in the side room to catch him at work. And it taught me an important lesson – don't ever try to beat the house at games with cards, shells, dice or chips 'cos it won't happen.

Chapter 10

CAMPING IN CHELMSFORD

Despite being dubbed the "dullest and most stupid place on earth" by Charles Dickens way back in 1835, when he couldn't find a Sunday newspaper, Chelmsford was now firmly established as my beat, the place where I would, without fear or favour, uncover the truth and expose skulduggery, while still covering things like the Conservative Christmas Bazaar which was a top notch event held in the town's Corn Exchange and supported by the great, good and, most importantly, wealthiest Tories in town.

Politically the county town of Essex was a safe Conservative seat and when I say safe I mean safe. It had its first Tory MP in 1885 and has stayed that way, apart from brief spells when the Unionist Party won in both 1910 and 1922 and the Commonwealth Party got in in 1945, through to the present day.

Although I was too young to vote, that privilege wouldn't come until the 1970 General Election, I knew that Norman St John Stevas was the town's elected representative although I didn't know whether to believe the gossip that he was homosexual; something that would remain illegal until

1967. He was certainly a dandy who camped it up in the finest no doubt bespoke suits and with the most affected mannerisms; it was enough to put the willies up a young man who didn't really understand anything about gay love but was familiar with the hilarious camp duo Julian and Sandy in the radio show *Round The Horne* and their version of the gay slang called polari.

Much later in life I learned from a friend who worked at the BBC during the 1960s that the reason why these two extravagantly camp characters were able to get away with their innuendo-ridden dialogue on the radio was because none of the corporation's power brokers and censors were prepared to own up to knowing what any of it meant for fear of being branded gay.

My only previous encounter with a homosexual had been when I was hitch-hiking to the Midlands to see relatives just after I left school. The man who picked me up in his flashy silver Bentley, grinned at me before making a sly move for my thigh as we sped along. I responded by picking up my rucksack and slamming it down as hard I could on his arm. He yelped and braked in the same movement before abruptly changing his travel plans so that they no longer included me.

There were rumours around town that a successful local builder named Barry Patience was gay but the six foot blonde Adonis only crossed my radar as the man who sponsored the very successful Saracens Sunday football team – there was talk of these amateur players being paid by Patience – and, more impressively, as the man who knew a Beatle.

His Brickey Building Company had been hired to work on Ringo Starr's house in Weybridge and in the summer of 1965, in the Tuesday edition of the *Newsman*, we had the exclusive story of what we dubbed "Ringo's Hush-Hush Trip To Chelmsford." It was complete with a photo of Ringo Starr "going into a house in Victoria Crescent" which I presumed was where Patience lived and we added that the Beatles' drummer was booked to have dinner at the Saracen's Head with his "partner in a building firm" which would have cost one of them, unless they went Dutch, just over 18s. (90p) although they could have gone to the County Hotel and had a meal for 14s (73p).

Oddly Patience's name was not mentioned in the story despite the fact we all knew he was Starr's business partner, but we did include the hotel manager saying, "The police have asked us to keep Ringo's visit very quiet to avoid fans turning up" while the police reassuringly added, "We shan't take any action unless it's necessary."

While St John Stevas never sent me a note (why would he write to a lanky, morose greasy-haired teenager?) he apparently wrote all his personal correspondence in purple ink and was also prone to lapse into Latin at the drop of a hat which, fortunately, he never did when I was around to report what he said. Nevertheless his speeches at the annual bazaar, and everywhere else, were still long, effusive and frankly boring but I was learning that this was something I should come to expect from politicians whether national or local.

What was weird was that Chelmsford, which had never seen a Labour MP in all its long life, had a plethora of Labour Mayors throughout the sixties which said something that I didn't really understand about politics. But as I couldn't vote, I really didn't care who ran what.

But the local Labour Party were not totally overwhelmed by their more established rivals and in 1966 they held their own Christmas Bazaar at the Corn Exchange and invited

Margaret Jay, wife of former civil servant turned journalist Peter Jay and the daughter of the then Chancellor of the Exchequer and future Prime Minister James Callaghan, to open the show.

Such was my ignorance of, or indifference to, politics that I rather hoped Mrs Jay might be the wife of Peter Jay of the Jaywalkers who had famously toured with The Beatles in 1963 but sadly it didn't turn out that way. My continuing ignorance of the nation's affairs meant that I didn't know or care that the Tory Government, and a man called Lord Beeching in particular, had set about cutting railway lines throughout Britain and that those cuts meant that I could no longer go by train in Essex from Witham to Maldon or Wivenhoe to Brightlingsea. Funnily enough it made little difference to my life as none of these places were on my radar.

I was focussed on Chelmsford where we had a High Street that offered major national chains such as Woolworths with its pick'n'mix sweets and dodgy Embassy cover version records, Marks & Spencer, Sainsbury's and Freeman Hardy & Willis who sold shoes to both proper grown-ups and hip young things like me.

Nearby was the ironmongers Grippers but as I still lived at home where my father was the so-called handyman – he was a skilled craftsman with what was known as a 'Birmingham screwdriver' (a hammer) - I had no knowledge of or interest in anything 'handy'. The grocers Luckin Smith operated an innovative cash system whereby your money was put in a metal cylinder and sent flying across the store on a high wire to the great cash desk in the sky where somebody sorted out your change and sent it whizzing back down to you – fabulous fun even for a sophisticated young man-about-town like me.

In Clarkes the stationers, whose shop was on a strange island in the High Street and involved climbing narrow stairs to get to the upper floors, you made your choice from a range of fountain pens (Parker were the bee's knees) with a selection of nibs – fine, extra fine, medium and broad – plus the ink that took your fancy. There was blue, black, blue-black and, I recall buying it once for a laugh, green. I never came across Norman St John Stevas' favourite purple – presumably it wasn't made by Quink and only available in fashionable London stores frequented by fops, dandies or Tory MPs.

The town's biggest shops were both locally owned department stores. Bonds opened in 1870 but it was some years later when my mother took me there for tea (or a milkshake) and scone (or cream cake). It was a fancy store where I sensed you had to be quiet and it had a fascinating display of stained glass panels in the windows on the first floor which overlooked the High Street. Opposite was the rival store Bolingbroke and Wenley which dated back even earlier to 1846 and had a splendid arcade running through the middle which you weren't allowed to cycle down. But of course we young rascals did whenever there was nobody around to put a stop to our childish pranks.

This was the time when the High Street was open to traffic - albeit only one way, down from the Shire Hall - which was also allowed to park on either side of the road where there were few if any parking restrictions although yellow parking lines were gradually being introduced in Britain in the 1960s. It was also the main route for cyclists leaving the Marconi and Hoffman works and at lunch time and late afternoon the High Street was like a scene from the Tour De France as bicycles weaved their way between the cars and buses.

On a very bad day the traffic, already coping with a plethora of bikes plus the pedestrian hordes of shoppers, children and workers, might also have to contend with the odd cow, sheep or pig (and maybe even a horse) as animals planned their great escape (sans motorbike) from the new livestock market in Victoria Road.

Although it wasn't a particularly big town, the people of Chelmsford seemed to know how to drink. It was a place that was awash with pubs or maybe it was just that I was mixing with journos who were notoriously heavy drinkers and liked to mix and match their hostelries to suit each and every occasion.

In the High Street there was the Queen's Head, a pub that dated back to 1876, and the Saracens Head, which began life as far back as 1591, while Springfield Road had a brewery with its own pub, both run by Grays. But it was Tindal Street – a small cut-through (named after the town's local judge who made good) that ran parallel to the High Street which took you from London Road to the Corn Exchange - that was the toast of the town. Even as a teetotaller it was still one of my favourite streets not least because there were more pubs per yard of pavement than any other street I had ever come across.

It was known as Back street – presumably as it was at the back of the High Street - and it was an education to stroll up there and peer into the Dolphin, Spotted Dog, Judge Tindal's Tavern and the White Hart before reaching the Golden Lion in Tindal Square which involved passing the Bell car park which was the site of another long-gone pub, The Bell. It was a colourful, noisy bustling side street in which local seed merchants Cramphorns had a shop and grain store, where on a good day you could spot a rodent or two. A bit further up there was Pope & Smith, the town's legendary sports shop launched by Essex cricketers Dudley Pope and Peter Smith, who also played for England.

At the other end of town there was, for the well-dressed up-to-date reporter, Mintz and Davis, our one and only real boutique which sold what we considered to be dapper and trendy menswear. There were proper denim jeans, the latest Ben Sherman and Fred Perry shirts, a range of off-the-peg suits and Denson shoes which ranged from two-tone brothel creepers to the sharpest winkle-pickers and trendy Chelsea boots.

I spent many a long hour being kitted out in this town centre store which was piled so high with 'schmutter' that the staff were forced to climb step-ladders to get to the top shelves. I didn't go in for anything too garish you under-stand because I was a professional but everything I bought was always, to my mind, modern and eye-catching - al-though my father was less convinced and preferred a reg-ular tweed jacket or cardigan and trousers bought from the likes of Fosters, Burton's or John Collier, the famous 'fifty bob tailors'. In fact he favoured anything that had enough pockets to take his pipe and smoker's tool kit which con-sisted of a tobacco pouch, matches, pipe cleaners and an all-in-one tool with a knife, a tamper and spike for sticking somewhere.

Although Chelmsford was my stomping ground there was other stuff going on in the bigger world and some of it rubbed off on me as I kept an ear to the ground. I knew that Labour's Harold Wilson had ended 13 years of Tory rule in the 1964 General Election, and replaced Sir Alec Douglas-Home as Prime Minister while, of course, Chelmsford re-mained a Tory stronghold.

Chapter 11

GOALS AND GAOLS

Given half a chance any provincial journalist worth his or her salt would find a way of turning a major national news story into a local scoop even if the connection was tenuous. If the story was good enough we would expand the Chronicle's circulation area by many a mile to make the link plausible.

In 1965 West Ham United - based in East London about 30 miles away from Chelmsford – became the second English team (after Tottenham) to win a European football trophy when they won the European Cup Winners Cup at Wembley. And the fact that Chelmsford's very own Geoff Hurst was in the team turned it into a "local boy hits the big time" story.

A year earlier I had gone to my first Wembley Cup Final when West Ham qualified for the '65 European competition. I went with a couple of school mates who were Southerners and Hammers fans so, with opponents Preston North End leading 2-1 at half time, I was moved to bet 2 bob (10 pence) that they would hold on and win.

I was not quite a Northerner but as a Midlander I felt

obliged to support any team from north of Watford, particularly one that boasted a big brute of a centre-forward
named Alex Dawson, who was known as 'The Black Prince'
despite being neither black nor royal. Sadly my new favourites didn't hold out as West Ham scored in the last minute to
win 3-2 and I saw my first exciting foray into the world of
gambling end as a miserable and expensive failure.

In fact this had been my second visit to the famous stadium as my father had taken me to see England - with a
young Duncan Edwards (20) and an old Stanley Matthews
(42) in the team (the veteran could've been the youngster's
father for God's sake) - play against Scotland in April 1957.
In fact it was Edwards who scored the winning goal in a
2-1 England victory after Scotland had led for over an hour.

While all this was going on Chelmsford's own New
Writtle Street football ground was reduced to what we
called "a battle ground" as, under the headline "Riot At
City Ground", we carried the story of two (or maybe three)
youths invading the pitch after a dull goalless draw with
Wellington, which later became part of Telford new town.
The story explained that the whole thing "looked like a
scene after a Latin-American game."

But it wasn't all punch-ups and mayhem as Chelmsford
Borough Council decided that the town needed more parking spaces for its growing number of car owners and two
car parks were opened at the end of 1965. As a result you
could park in Glebe Road for 6d (2½p) an hour but – and
this was value for money – it was just 1s (5p) for a whole
day's long-term stay in Rainsford Road.

With the editorship of a local newspaper went the opportunity to abuse that power and slip in a story that was
a blatant plug for family or friends although the average
reader in the street was never the wiser. A major *Newsman*

feature focussed on a young lady called Carol who had seemingly returned from her honeymoon to begin work in the new family florist business in New Street.

The story went on to explain that "when the shop opened it gave some 6000 workers from Marconi and Hoffmann factories a very pleasant surprise" - this certainly came as a surprise to me as I wasn't sure how important a flower shop was to those who toiled in the local factories. However there was one thing that the story didn't point out about Carol and that was that her new husband was Rodney Andrews, son of the paper's editor and a staff reporter.

To the best of my recollection there was never what you would call a crime wave in Chelmsford. There was a bunch of usual suspects who did some burglary, shoplifting, breaking and entering and got involved in the odd scuffle but major bank jobs and post office raids, when they did happen, were carried out by out-of-town villains who made a quick getaway, usually up the A12 back to the 'Smoke'.

PC Dave Perry was the victim of one gang who came riding into Chelmsford to break into one of the High Street banks in a night-time raid. When he disturbed them he was beaten unconscious and left in a deserted car park area at the back of Bonds department store. He eventually managed to crawl a few hundred yards and radio for help before being taken to hospital.

Impressively the villains were arrested within a day – and eventually sent to prison - while Perry, an amiable fresh-faced rookie officer, made a steady recovery but his ordeal shook not just the police but the whole town.

I always got on well with Perry and some years later, after I had joined the neighbouring *Braintree & Witham Times* (where I learnt to drive at the paper's expense), our paths crossed again when the company car I was driving one evening was in collision in New London Road with a car which pulled out of a side turning into my path.

It was a clear case of the other driver being at fault as it was my right of way and the policeman who arrived to sort out the debris was Perry who turned out to be ever helpful. Coincidentally I also knew the other driver as he was the landlord of the Marsham Arms, a public house I used to frequent for lunch with colleagues.

After the crash, me and the ex-publican both gave our details to Perry and made our way home although I was off work for a couple of days with badly bruised ribs and hands – the result of being a smartarse and not wearing a seatbelt, which was fitted but not required by law to be worn in those days. Even though seat belts had been installed in cars under the law since 1965 it would be a further 18 years before it became compulsory for them to be worn ... and then only by drivers.

Later Dave Perry (we were on first name terms by now) visited me at home and asked me how fast I had been travelling and we quickly agreed that, as it was a 30mph limit, I had been doing 29mph. However he then pointed out that an off-duty policeman – somebody I knew but didn't like and who didn't get on with my father either – was prepared to give evidence that I was exceeding the speed limit.

This was when I discovered that evidence from a police officer – even an off duty one – was considered to be more than acceptable to the court (and insurance companies presumably) than that of an honest to goodness journalist as he was a 'professional' who could, even though he was walking on the pavement, give an accurate estimate of a speed of a moving vehicle.

Despite the fact that the other driver had cut across my path, and because I might just have been speeding a bit, I could be deemed to be something called a "contributory factor" and it could result in both of us being prosecuted. The ever-helpful Perry recommended that as nobody was seriously hurt, he was happy to write the whole thing off (less paperwork no doubt) and leave it to the insurance companies to sort out. It would be another ten years or more before I got nabbed for real in a speed trap and even longer before I spoke to the off-duty copper again.

The Marsham Arms had become our new Friday lunch-time venue in the aftermath of what we dubbed the 'Canton incident.'

The Canton restaurant in Baddow Road was one of the first Chinese eating houses to open in Chelmsford and was a favourite haunt for me and a few editorial colleagues on a Friday after the newspaper came out.

These were the early days of exotic Oriental cuisine coming to the county town and it has to be said that we weren't overly adventurous in our choices; it was usually sweet and sour pork or egg foo yung with fried rice followed by banana fritters with ice cream. The even less adventurous amongst us settled on an omelette and chips Chinese style – bloody enormous!

However, when the Canton was taken to court after mice droppings and grease deposits were found by health inspectors, things changed. The five Chinese proprietors all pleaded guilty, were fined £35 each and, while they promised to put things right, that didn't make it right for one of my dining companions who, being a touch on the squeamish side, decided that we should never eat there again.

So off we went to the pub run by the man who would later appear in my headlights. And here, in the Waterhouse Lane hostelry, we indulged in the safest fare on offer - sausages, chips and peas or burgers (no buns), chips and peas. All

hearty English fare a million miles away from all that foreign stuff.

While we had Vicky as the town's go-to cat burglar, there
were a few others who worked on the wrong side of the
law. The aptly named Rob, for instance, combined window
cleaning with thieving but could never work out why he
was caught when women reported their jewellery going
missing just after Rob had been around with his chamois.
He also fancied himself as a bit of a boxer and the story that
raced around town like wildfire was about him turning on
a bus driver after they had a row over whose right of way
it was – Rob's or the bus'- at the entrance to the bus station.

While Rob postured, shadow-boxed and generally
taunted the driver to get out of his cab and get a 'seeing to',
the driver apparently climbed out of his bus, walked over
to Rob and, without uttering a single word, smacked him in
the mouth before getting back into his bus and driving off.

One of the more violent crimes involved a waitress in
Lyon's tea house in the High Street who was attacked by
her ex-boyfriend with a large carving knife. She was badly
injured, he was arrested, charged and sentenced and in
July 1965 I covered the case and my story appeared in the
paper with a headline which referred to Mick the attacker
as 'killer' – even though nobody actually died.

Over a decade later I was on a crowded platform at
Chelmsford railway station when Mick, who I had not seen
since his court appearance for the knife attack – when he
was sent to prison for a good few years - appeared up the
stairs and shouted "Hi, Brian". I turned and, unable to remember his name, blurted out "Hello, Killer" in a voice
loud enough to scare away a whole host of commuters. He
didn't seem overly bothered about it and halfway through
our chat on the train his name came back to me and I then

made a great point of calling him "Mick" as often as possible just in case he turned nasty - again!.

Most of the town's regular villains were well-known to both the press and the police but while we were grateful for the odd tip-off about an arrest, we never reciprocated by acting as informers and 'grassing up' anyone unless it was as an actual witness to a crime. However this high moral stance on my part won me no points with one of the town's most persistent and least clever crooks.

Barry had a history with the long arm of law, having been picked up and deposited in the nick so often they might have named one of the police station's cells in his honour. Sadly he was not a criminal genius. Two of his finest moments came when a fellow lodger in his digs mentioned over breakfast that he had a shirt just like the one Barry was wearing. After Barry told him "not any more you haven't", the master criminal was picked up for the theft of a shirt.

Not content with this moment of madness, Barry popped into the Chelmsford Museum in Oaklands Park, forced open a display cabinet and helped himself to a selection of Victorian coins. Armed with his newly acquired cash in hand, he went into a nearby boozer where he handed over the antique coins in exchange for a pint. That too brought the local fuzz a-running and he was eventually sentenced to 12 months.

Unfortunately Barry was also prone to the odd spot of violence as I saw for myself at the nearby Springfield Lyons venue during a dance night featuring a local band. I went downstairs to the toilets where I came across Barry accusing some kid of calling him a c*** while holding him in a choke hold which was slowly turning the lad's face purple. The teenager, even though he was struggling to talk, was still desperate in his denial and after Barry and I had exchanged pleasantries - "Hi, Barry"; "Hello, Brian" that sort of thing - I went back to the dance floor.

A few minutes later the youngster came staggering up the stairs with blood pouring from his nose as a result of Barry banging his face into a porcelain wash basin. All I could think of saying was "So Barry didn't believe you then?" Not helpful but pithy and to the point, as was his response which sounded something like "Fftk othh."

All this Barry-centric activity sort of came to a head one Christmas Eve. Barry was keen to stay out of prison for at least one Christmas – he had done something like three on the trot in the nick – but he was wanted for trying to pass forged cheques around the town. I was passing through Tindal Square when I was stopped by one of the town force's least fine detective sergeants. He wanted to know if I had seen Barry anywhere as he was on the lookout for a Christmas collar.

Just as I was explaining that I hadn't seen him and wouldn't tell even if I had, Barry walked across the other side of the square and my eyes were automatically drawn to him. Then the detective turned and saw him too. He gave chase and caught up with Barry who was flung into the cells on remand until after the festive season was over – another not so jolly 12 days of Christmas for poor Baz.

In the New Year, Barry appeared in court and was sent to prison (again) and I thought nothing more about it until I was stopped in town by one of Barry's mates who told me that Barry was convinced I had grassed him up to the detective in Tindal Square and he was going to "see to me" when he got out. I told the messenger to go back and tell Barry that I hadn't said a thing.

The message came back that Barry wasn't convinced and as the time for his release came round, I was 'invited' to meet him in the grounds of Chelmsford Cathedral one autumn evening for a "shoot out" but without guns ... I hoped. We met in a scene similar a Western gunfight and, while I steeled myself for a thumping, I did my best to explain what had happened – how I hadn't said a word but just spotted him out of the corner of my eye which the DS had noticed, turned round and saw Barry for himself.

As I am still here to tell the tale with all my limbs and teeth intact, I obviously made a good job of convincing Barry of my innocence. But like all good villains he couldn't let it go with a friendly "sorry mate", but had to tell me that if I ever did anything like that again I would be in trouble. I left neither battered nor bruised but just a bit bewildered.

Chelmsford was overrun by journalists from Fleet Street in April 1965 when a team of prisoners from Chelmsford nick were 'let out' for a local football cup final played at Chelmsford City's ground. Special permission for the game to take place was granted by the Home Secretary and among the dignitaries in the crowd were some of our local magistrates who just might have been the ones who sent some of the prison team to do porridge.

It was my first experience of what we now know as a 'media frenzy' as reporters, photographers and TV crews fought for angles and exclusives – but no interviews. We carried a full page picture spread with all the prisoners' faces covered – this was before the arrival of pixelating which allows for the efficient blurring of faces and body parts - with a clumsily drawn white cross similar to the ones used in the ever popular 'Spot The Ball' competitions.

The prison team, which played in Division II of the Mid-Essex Combination League, won the cup, beating a side from the village of Thaxted 6-4 but that was not the end of it for the old lags XI. They were allowed back out the next year for another local cup final against Black Notley (who I would later play for with my brother) but this time they lost 3-2.

A few years later – in the late sixties - I played football in a pre-season friendly in Chelmsford prison when it was still called the County Jail and housed murderers and other serious criminals. It would later become 'home' to Arsenal and England footballers Tony Adams and Ian Wright and was also the location for a Sex Pistols live album, a gig by the Stranglers and the film of the TV series *Porridge*.

It is a great ugly building with high walls (obviously) that was opened in 1830 at a cost of £57,000 and was situated in Springfield Road in what was described at the time as "an airy and pleasant situation." The gates were really something to be behold – huge wooden things with a smaller doorway for visitors to pass through, both as secure as you always hoped they would be. It was all grey, as grey as a squirrel (a grey one obviously) and inside it was an equally desolate, soul-destroying place and reminded me of a medieval castle as it echoed with the sound of heavy boots on stone floors, keys locking and unlocking cells along with shouts from the inmates who were locked up.

We had to go through a bit of security to get in; a not very thorough body search and a cursory look in our kit bags to ensure there were no cakes, files, fags or choccies - but thankfully no rubber gloves or sniffer dogs were involved. Those would come later for me after touring Europe with the Rolling Stones in 1973! In the nick we got changed for the game under the gaze of a couple of warders who ensured all our personal possessions were locked away safely in the changing room while joking that there were "thieves about."

The great thing about the game itself was that you could

pretty much get away with murder (not literally of course) as you could push, kick and foul as much as you liked because if the prisoners reacted (and some had a natural instinct towards violence) they were nabbed by the referee/ warder and then lost their cigarette and chocolate privileges. Happily for us they gritted their teeth and took it like the men they were ... and we won but, more importantly, nobody ever came looking for us.

Some years later I went back to Chelmsford prison but this time it was to play cricket for a Press team against inmates in a one-off limited overs one-day decider. We won handsomely but the eye-opener was seeing a few 'trustee' prisoners seated on tiered benches as spectators with a couple separated off with their own guards. When I asked what it was all about I was told they were the sex offenders and they had to be kept away from the other prisoners who, in the words of one warder, "would take their eyes out with a plastic spoon."

Pretty frightening stuff to hear on a quiet Sunday afternoon when the only other noise was an echoing shout from a distant cell window of "hit the f*****g ball." Obviously it was from a frustrated connoisseur of the "gentleman's game."

Chapter 12

PIRATES AND PORNOGRAPHERS

Rather cheekily setting ourselves up as judge and jury, the 'Round the Sound Track' team (just me and Andrews Jnr. actually) had the cheek at the start of 1966 to invent our own 1965 pop awards where we went out on a limb and gave the prize for Top Group (British & International) to The Beatles and decided that 'You've Lost That Lovin' Feeling' (by The Righteous Brothers) and 'I Can't Get No Satisfaction' (by The Rolling Stones) tied as Best Single. Bizarrely, we gave Top International Male Singer to P J Proby who had notched up just one top ten hit when we could have gone for American stars such Roy Orbison, Bob Dylan or even Elvis himself.

An all-important football match took place in January 1966 when an *Essex Chronicle* team took on Chelmsford Police Station's finest.

A photo of the *Chronicle* XI made it into the *Newsman* and included me, Martin Rogers, Lou Cummins, and Ray Horsnall alongside assorted printers. I put down the fact that we lost 2-1 to an attempt on our part to improve press/police relations.

In February 1966, in line with the paper's policy of trying to keep everyone happy, I wrote a feature on the face-lift that owner George Watkins planned for his Pavilion cinema. He was intending to change (nay improve) the viewing habits of the town and introduce films of opera, ballet and drama for one night each month. He also announced his plan for a new hot-air central heating system that was guaranteed to warm the cinema in just 30 minutes.

A year later Watkins introduced the town's first cinema smoking ban when he announced that there would be no smoking on the left hand side of the gangway in the cinema and that the ashtrays would be removed.

After narrowly losing to a Chelmsford Police X1, *Essex Chronicle* photographer (and goalie) Ray Horsnall (right) decided to drench me with water from a chamber pot he just happened to have with him

It seemed like a fanciful idea unless he was going to introduce fans to keep the smoke over on the right hand side.

While the paper was notoriously mean with by-lines and credits, in May 1966 I did manage to get another B.S. (in bold) on a review of *The Beggar's Opera* performed by Chelmsford Technical High School. As the 'ballad opera' by John Gay from 1728 was something I had never seen or even heard of, I'm not sure how I qualified to review this EXCEPT that it was put on by my old grammar school and that seemed to be the way it worked - Cummins covered a lot of performances by his old school King Edward V1 grammar while I did my old alma mater. Unqualified as I was, I described the whole thing as an "ambitious attempt" (what did I know?) which "came off very well." High praise indeed.

For no particular reason other than curiosity about what it all meant and entailed, I made a third visit to Wembley in June 1966 during the World Cup finals when, as some sort of Billy-no-mates, I took myself off to watch France play Mexico in a match in Group One which also included England and Uruguay. Having decided that I had nothing better to do on a summer's evening – despite being available but for some reason shunned by Chelmsford's seemingly overly choosy females - I travelled to London and bought a ticket (along with 69,000 other people) to watch a tedious 1-1 draw which resulted in neither side going any further in the competition.

At the end of the following month England found themselves in the World Cup final facing West Germany and with local Chelmsford lad Geoff Hurst in the team this was an excuse for the *Chronicle* to go to town to celebrate the man who helped bring the Jules Rimet trophy home. But oddly there was very little celebration.

The July 29 issue – the day before the final – carried one World Cup related advert which pronounced "Fine For The Final … but what if it's wet." It came from a company in far off Romford that had supplied 22 miles of fibre glass and aluminium sheeting to go round the Wembley roof but there was not a single word on the sports pages about the match.

The following week's edition – August 5 – carried a photo of Hurst under the headline "No Home Town Cheers for Geoff" and the story that nobody was around when he visited his parent's home in Chelmsford on the day after the final – presumably clutching his winner's medal. At the same time the chairman of Chelmsford City football club asked if the local council planned any celebration and added, "If they haven't then we will."

At the end of September – when there were still no reports of a celebration – a letter came in to the Chronicle from 24 locals sports fans who were "disgusted at the failure of the local authorities to recognise the World Cup feats of Geoff Hurst". A follow-up letter then suggested that the West Ham player be given the freedom of the Borough.

But there still seemed little appetite or incentive to go ahead with any celebratory event for the only player to have scored a hat-trick in the 36 year history of the World Cup although the paper's end of year sports round-up in December did acknowledge the former Rainsford schoolboy as "truly one of Chelmsford's most famous sporting exports."

As for me, I watched the match at home with my father as my brother got together with a bunch of football team mates to watch the game in their local club house and my mother was somewhere else – perhaps shopping, taking tea or at the cinema – anywhere that wasn't showing a football match. Oddly I don't recall there being any great excitement in our household at the result as both my father and I were pragmatic people not given to shows of great emotion at the outcome of sporting events ... not even when Villa beat Birmingham – after all it was still only a game. I did get excited as a 10 year old when Villa won the FA cup (the last time they did) but after that (coupled with a smack round the ear from granddad for being noisy) common sense took over.

1966 also brought about a story that captured the headlines both nationally and locally and it was one that was played out in the Assize Court in Chelmsford and was a case I covered from my privileged and hard-fought-for position in the court's press box.

It was the time when pirate radio stations were making all the noise and attracting all the youngsters by playing non-stop pop music. Radio Caroline and Radio London, both moored and broadcasting three miles off the British coast and in international waters, were the leading 'pirates' although smaller stations with lofty ambitions soon followed.

Oliver Smedley launched a pirate station called Radio Atlanta which over time became Radio Caroline South. He entered into takeover talks with Reginald Calvert, the manager of Screamin' Lord Sutch and the pop group The Fortunes, who had launched Radio City, but things turned sour between them after a row over a transmitter and unpaid bills.

In June, Calvert turned up late at night and uninvited at Smedley's home in the Essex village of Wendens Ambo, near Saffron Walden and about 30 miles from Chelmsford. Aware that Calvert was angry and reputed to have a gun, Smedley armed himself with his own shotgun before open-

ing the door. In the ensuing fracas Calvert was shot dead
and Smedley charged with his murder

The local magistrate's court reduced the charge to manslaughter and Smedley appeared before us all at the Essex
Assizes in October where he pleaded not guilty. As the
story unfolded the national press came up with headlines
such as "Pop Pirate Chief Shot Dead" and I was in the midst
of a major national murder (alright, manslaughter) trial.
The court was overrun by so-called 'proper' journalists
from London who made all sorts of pompous and arrogant
claims for seats in the tiny press box where we locals sat
week after week.

They got short shrift from the likes of Vosper and Rouse
and we all sat our ground for the duration of the trial which
ended with Smedley being found not guilty. The jury ac-
cepted his claim of self-defence, no doubt aided by the
judge Mr Justice Stevenson telling them in his summing up
that Calvert's behaviour that night was "very much like the
conduct of a lunatic."

A year later, in 1967, and much to my annoyance, pirate
radio was killed off once and for all by the Labour Government of the day and the BBC set up Radio 1 as some sort
of half-hearted panacea to soften the blow for a horde of
pop-hungry teenagers.

When the grocers Caters arrived in Chelmsford to open
the town's first supermarket, they did it in fine style. There
was music, balloons and young girls giving away treats up
and down the High Street. All these celebrations meant
very little to us editorially but it was a major boon to the
paper's advertising income when the London-based company opened its doors on the ground floor of the brand new
eight storey Cater House they erected on the site of an old
Wesleyan Church.

They advertised job opportunities alongside food offers but it was still slightly odd that the county town only got its first supermarket four years after the rival Tesco company had opened its first Essex supermarket in the much smaller nearby town of Maldon. But what Maldon did not get slap dab in its town centre was a tower block of offices (once home to the local tax authority) which ranked as the equal second tallest building in Chelmsford.

Melbourne Court, standing at 14 storeys, remained the biggest but Cater House joined Rivers House in Springfield Road (the home to the Essex Rivers Authority, built in 1964) in the runners up spot. Incidentally one of the Authority's senior directors was the father of a school friend and he went by what we thought was the hilarious and wholly appropriate name of Hugh Fish.

The summer of 1966 saw John Rice, the ex-copper who co-owned the R&B coffee bar, arrested in blazing sunshine on Carnival Day (July 2) as he dodged through the crowds to try and get away from the police. Just before he was caught, he threw his wallet into the river and after it was recovered, he and an accessory were charged with being "in possession of papers resembling revenue papers" -- forged driving licences, insurance certificates and a Kent Constabulary warrant card.

He and his sidekick, an artist who was involved in the actual forgery of the documents, both pleaded guilty at Essex Assizes in November and, while Rice got two years and his side-kick three years, I got a cursory nod of acknowledgement from the man in the dock who had made me countless coffees.

Sentencing, Mr Justice Lang said, "The dangerous part of this conspiracy was the combination of an ex-police officer, running a cafe that had at some stage been slightly disreputable, and a particularly skilful commercial artist." That was my favourite hang-out and here was a judge who had never set foot in the place slagging it off.

There were a couple of houses of ill repute in Chelmsford back in the sixties and although I knew where they were, I only took a professional interest. Soliciting and living off immoral earnings were both against the law as was keeping a brothel but I was never sure how organised our very own local bordellos were. I knew some of the girls by sight and while they were tempting in a bawdy sort of way they were, in the main, just plain scary.

Some of the local coppers who spent their time on the beat confirmed that one establishment was in New London Road and another along Rainsford Road but it seemed to us on the paper to be more a case of a few local girls putting it about for a few extra bob than an organised prostitution ring. However, as I never went to either one, nor to a local nurses' hostel where favours were rumoured to be offered or returned, I didn't have enough evidence for an exposé of the town's seedy underbelly where I could name and shame any local dignitaries or businessmen. It was clear I was not cut out for a job on the News of the World.

New Street ran from the local police station as far as the giant Hoffman factory where my wife's mother and aunt both worked during WWII. It wasn't an elegant street and ranked as a bit of an eyesore and, for me, the two stand-out premises were the William IV pub and Chamberlain's joke and toy store.

The pub was a strange building, which I think went back to the days of horse-drawn coaches as it had a wide archway at the front which opened out into a courtyard. In the 1960s, the arched entrance was home to an old crone who sat herself on a chair and abused passers-by with a selection of colourful insults, some of which turned a young man's cheeks red with embarrassment. I think somebody told me she was called Queenie but I never found out who she was or who she belonged to as I always made a point of crossing the road before I got within earshot of her tirade.

Whether or not there was actually a Mister Chamberlain I never knew but the shop that bore his name was something of an Aladdin's cave, full of toys, models and jokes. But, as I found out from the local boys in blue, there was something more sinister going on under the counter. This was the home of Chelmsford's pornography business.

Pornography was all a bit of a mystery to me. I had looked at the odd copy of Spick and Span magazine and the even more risqué *Kamera* magazine featuring the handiwork of esteemed glamour photographer (that's what they called nude photography in the 1950 and 1960s) Harrison Marks, but that was just young ladies in various stages of undress and there was never a man to be seen.

But what was on offer at Chamberlain's was a whole different kettle of fish and because of that it was regularly raided by local detectives who took away envelopes full of black and white photographs which they happily shared with their mates and trusted members of the Fourth Estate.

This as it turned out was proper 'porn' featuring men and women fully naked with all their bits out on display and doing things to each other which, although I had often (too often some would say) read about, had never actually seen captured in lurid close up in 5" x 3" snap shots ... and from such interesting angles!

As the bloke who ran, and I presumed owned, Chamberlain's was never arrested, charged or brought before the court, I can only assume he was let off with a warning and on condition that the police could keep (and share as they saw fit) any stashes of porn they collected from him during their regular visits.

Opposite Chamberlain's was a short terrace of shops with flats above and here there was a men's barbers (they weren't hairdressers back then), an arty-farty shop selling pottery and homemade jewellery and, most excitingly, a brand new boutique. Apart from Mintz & Davis and a small shop in Barrack Square, there was a dearth of outlets in Chelmsford for a dedicated follower of fashion such as myself. And I embraced this new one with enthusiasm especially when I was sent off to create a half-page advertorial feature to go with the half-page advertisement the shop's owner had taken in the paper.

Back then if a company or business bought a full-page advert, they got a page of advertorial, for a half page you got half as much and so on downwards. The downside was that it fell to us reporters to create the flimflam or tosh that was supposed to promote the business but normally it read like a PR handout and was about as interesting as a politician's speech.

The only upside, if it was a boutique or perhaps a bike shop or maybe a restaurant, was the possibility of getting something for free or on the cheap further down the line – depending on whether the business appreciated your prose or if they actually stayed open long enough to show their appreciation.

Chapter 13

WHATEVER HAPPENED TO BOUTIQUE EDDIE?

The new Towngear shop opened in July 1966 and was run by Eddie with help from his partner Sylv. They were not married which was not relevant to the story but brought some much needed spice into my life as every other 'old' couple I knew were husband and wife. He was as smooth as milk chocolate with a tan to match plus a slightly greying quiff, his shirt was always open a few buttons too many and he wore a flashy gold wrist bracelet.

At the wrong side of thirty, he wasn't quite hip but was probably sophisticated and his new shop boasted just a few 'select' items of menswear which made it classier than Mintz's which was stacked to the rafters with folded jeans, shirts and endless shoe boxes but, it has to be said, always had a lot more customers.

My advertorial piece on the boutique appeared under the heading (not written by me) "Hey Cats! a boutique that swings for you" with the sub-heading 'Carnaby Street comes to town' and explained that the owner was 35 year-old Londoner Eddie Ayley who said that during his days at the heart of London's fashion world he had dealt with The Rolling Stones and The Beatles. It crossed my mind that this was something every boutique owner claimed in the sixties..

I went on to explain that Towngear was "a male boutique where the long and short haired youth of Chelmsford can go along and buy whatever they want, however extravagant and outlandish it maybe." Despite struggling to fill the half page with copy, I didn't see fit to mention that I had my own Carnaby Street experience when I was in Irvine Sellars shop and bumped into the least famous Walker Brother - drummer Gary Leeds - who was buying a fancy shirt with a tab collar. Needless to say I bought the same shirt!

After my editorial effort I spent quite a lot of time in Eddy's shop – and did get discount on quite a few items of funky (in my eyes) clothing – and it was a mighty shock when I called at the police station one morning to be told the shop had been burgled overnight and all the stock stolen. When I went to see him to give him my condolences on his loss (and get a quote to go with the story) he took me into the tiny kitchen and held out a sizeable sealed brown envelope.

He asked me to take it, hide it, never open it and only bring it back after the police had finished their investigation. For some reason I agreed and in true James Bond fashion, tucked the envelope down the back of my trousers, under my shirt and jacket, and walked off pretty smart-ish before the CID came a-calling. A couple of days later I went back to give Eddie his envelope only to find a very smart white Jaguar parked outside the shop and a short-ish but very wide man standing in (and filling) the open doorway.

He asked (not very politely it has to be said) who I was

and what I wanted and as I stammered that I was there to return something to Eddie, the man himself emerged looking a little paler than usual and not quite so self-assured. Once Eddie gave the OK, the 'doorman' moved over a little and let me squeeze into the shop.

There were a couple more well-dressed and imposing blokes inside who looked me up and down as Eddie took me into the kitchen area where I handed over the envelope. When I asked (quietly) what was going on and why was there a scary man on the door, he told me that I didn't need to know who it was and that I shouldn't hang about too long.

I looked around the shop and noticed that there wasn't anything there – no clothes, no pictures on the wall, none of the little pieces of pottery, not even the kettle and mugs in the kitchen … the place was bare. I left and never saw Eddie ever again.

The shop never reopened and the police never caught anyone for the break-in and I never found out what was in the envelope. Putting two and two together I decided that the break-in and 'theft' was an inside job and, as the shop never seemed to do a lot of business, probably some sort of insurance swindle.

The local detectives added to the mystery as they explained that they thought Eddie had some contacts with organised crime – maybe even the notorious Kray twins whose 'manor' was London's East End where Eddie Ayley told me he had grown up. It might be worth noting that the London extensions to the M1 motorway were under construction around this time and there were always lots of stories about criminals and concrete.

However, not everything was as exciting as a possible run-in with mobsters from the 'smoke' and in September I produced a caption story about the father of my best mate from school retiring from the Essex Police and emigrating to Australia to become a plumber. This exciting news went with a photo of the ex-copper packing boxes for the trip.

Less than a year later there came a riveting follow-up with the story that my old school pal whose family had gone to Oz, had received a telegram from Australia House saying there was a flight next day to Australia if he wanted to go. So off he flew to Melbourne and then on to Sydney to join his family and I didn't see him again until 20 years later when he returned on a visit. We got together and over dinner I discovered I had nothing in common any more with this bearded Grizzly Adams character who had seemingly left his wife and children to live a nomadic life in the Tasmanian outback as a follower of Nostradamus.

The excitement of working on a local paper continued with a story for all the local gardeners and allotment owners which appeared under the heading "Special Prize For A Giant Onion." At the combined Great and Little Leighs Autumn show the star attraction and overall winner was an onion weighing in at 2.5 lbs (1.13kgs) but sadly there was no photograph to back it up.

The now familiar bold B.S. appeared again in October when the Sandon Players presented Bertold Brecht's *The Good Woman (of Setzuan)* as part of Chelmsford Cathedral Week. It suggested that I was there to enjoy all of the nearly two hours of the Chinese drama although I have no memory of ever seeing the play and what appeared in print seems to have been a straight lift from the programme notes. It featured under the headline: "Sandon Players Brilliant Production of Brecht's Long Play" and interestingly the following week a very long and flowing review of the play appeared from the pen of colleague Hemmings.

It was not unusual for us to skip a play or show and then rely on the programme notes or a bit of personal knowledge in order to file some relevant copy – and the secret was to always be positive. Remember nobody ever complained if you said nice things. This was a code that I took with me to *Melody Maker* when we did occasionally review albums without listening to them – it filled a hole at the bottom of the review page on press day – and then on to my days at EMI where heavy metal was something I never really took to. My plan was go along to the venue, make sure I said hello to the act's manager before the show and then skedaddle, vamoose, high tail it out of there as fast as possible before returning to the after-show party full of compliments.

On a more serious note, in October 1966 the whole country was on the alert for the man dubbed "Britain's Most Wanted Man" – double police murderer Harry Roberts - and we got in on the story with the headline 'Hunt For Roberts In Football Crowd.' The story confirmed that "detectives swooped" on Chelmsford City's New Writtle Street ground after a spectator reported that a man "very much like Roberts" was at the ground. He wasn't and Roberts was eventually arrested a month later and about 20 miles away in a wood in Bishops Stortford.

There was what we thought was a fun front page story in March 1967 which I had a hand in pulling together after a "near naked man" was chased through the local nurses' hostel in New London Road. We reported that he escaped through a window wearing a blue dressing gown, which he had stolen, and red socks (which we presumed were his own). There was a follow-up story a month later when he went back to the hostel, this time wearing just his underpants, but carrying his trousers. One of the nurses told us in all innocence that they planned to "booby-trap the place" in case of any further unwanted visits. We all thought he'd definitely go back one more time for that.

Playing for St Margarets – under the stewardship of *Chronicle* colleague Martin Rogers – meant that a report of our matches almost always appeared in the paper and as he ran four teams (there were two on both Saturday and Sunday) readers were given regular up-dates on our performances. It was all a perk of his job as assistant sports editor and in March 1967 I got an undistinguished mention in dispatches.

It was a game against the local Marconi company and the report confirmed that the "works outside left was sent off after 54 minutes followed five minutes later by St Margarets right back Brian Southall." But that wasn't the end of it as another Marconi player was sent off with me. I recall tackling the first guy enthusiastically (and fairly in my view) but he (over) reacted, hit me and was sent off. Five minutes later the first guy's brother came after me and tackled me most unfairly and when I turned on him to ask him to curb his ways, we had a bout of fisticuffs for which we were both sent off. We still had ten men to their nine but to no avail as the match ended all square at 1-1.

A later report about St Margarets reserves – I had been relegated by then because I often worked on a Saturday afternoon (the news didn't stop at the weekend) - confirmed an impressive 7-0 win with the final goal coming from the substitute who apparently only came on after "captain Brian Southall had been accidentally punched on the nose by his own goalkeeper" But was it an accident? Was I the popular skipper I thought I was?

We had a lengthy trial to cover at the Essex Assizes in April 1967 concerning the goings-on at the very dubious Leete Hotel in the nearby village of Writtle which was always rumoured to be a den of iniquity. The manager, the wonderfully named, James Goldie-Jones was finally convicted after over three hours of deliberation by the jury. He was sentenced to two years for forgery, demanding money (the princely sum of £2) with menaces and fraudulently obtaining money. One of the detectives involved in the case told the court that in the past year four men from the hotel had been arrested for dishonesty and he concluded that the hotel "was not a very desirable place."

It wasn't very local but in the summer of 1967, a brief war began on June 5 when Egypt closed the Straits of Tiran to Israeli shipping and the Israelis retaliated by attacking Egypt. A ceasefire was finally signed on June 11, by which time Israel had lost nearly 900 people and Egypt and its allies Syria and Jordan had suffered nearly 15,000 losses.

In the aftermath of the infamous Six Day War there was a huge surge of interest from young people – some were young Jewish teenagers while others were sixties hippies plus actors Bob Hoskins, Helen Mirren and Sigourney Weaver – all eager to volunteer to work on a kibbutz (a traditional agricultural community) in Israel to support the country.

In the midst of all this I was sent to the Israeli Consulate in Kensington (where travel documents were issued) to scout for any locals from Chelmsford who might be volunteering. I recall finding one guy who was from the area and he told me his story. It turned out that his mother lived in Writtle and they had lost touch over the years but after this meeting I was able to let her know her son was at least alive – if not altogether safe - and on his way to Israel.

Now my memory has it that I wrote this as an exclusive and interesting news story – an international event with a good local twist – but there is nothing in the files of either the *Chronicle* or *Newsman* to support my theory. Did it get dumped and 'spiked' (sub-editor's traditionally had a spike on a wooden base on their desk on which they stuck copy when it was finished or not used) or did I just imagine it all? Very odd and a mystery that I am unlikely ever to solve.

My continuing (very) loose association with the stars came to the fore in September 1967 when we managed to put together a story that Mick Jagger was looking for a new home in Essex. The rumour was that the Rolling Stone was going to pay £45,000 for New Riffhams, a 23 room Georgian mansion in Danbury, just three miles from Chelmsford. But of course, despite our front page headline, he didn't buy it (they never do) although a local lady insisted, "If Mick Jagger does come to live here I think people would take it in their stride. "

In the same month a man came to court after he had booked a non-existent band for a couple's wedding and was subsequently fined £5 for obtaining the £2 booking fee from the father of bride by false pretences. The father had done some research to try and find out if the band were any good or not and discovered that they didn't exist -- and this was before Google and the internet.

At the end of the year the editor who hired me was, to my mind, demoted to be editor of just the Chelmsford Newsman while a new editor was appointed for the *Essex Chronicle*. Was it office politics, had he ruffled too many feathers or just outstayed his welcome? I never did find out – because he never told me – but Andrews eventually left to lecture in journalism at Harlow College. And who did he teach? Well it could have been rock musicians Steve Harley and Mark Knopfler and music writer Charles Shaar Murray who all attended the college in the late sixties and early seventies.

Years later I would cross paths with two of those trainee journos. Steve Harley (and his band Cockney Rebel) was signed to EMI when I joined in 1974 and I eventually ended up working on his last couple of albums for the company and we remain close friends to this day.

Shaar Murray also came into my sights during his days with *New Musical Express* in the 1970s and 1980s when he worked alongside the likes of Julie Burchill, Nick Kent and Tony Parsons. My press office failed miserably to get him or any of his colleagues to cover acts such as Cliff Richard, Queen. Pink Floyd and Wings as the *NME* was not the paper for these commercial, multi-million selling acts once punk and new wave arrived on the scene, but they were not always content with just ignoring them – they did go out of their way to ridicule them and, on occasions, came near to libelling them.

As for Knopfler? Despite spending nearly 40 years in the music business I never met him and never knew he trained as a journalist.

One of the unwritten rules of journalism was that the writers wrote the words and the photographers took the pictures. It wasn't a hanging offence and I think we all belonged to the same union(s) but unless it was an emergency, and involved lives being saved or papers being published, we kept to our chosen areas of expertise. If they took a photo, they would get details of the subject and the event and pass it on so we could assemble it all into some sort of appropriate caption.

But there were exceptions and a football match in December 1967 was one of them. Chelmsford City and Oxford United had played out two 3-3 draws in the 1st round of the FA Cup and then met for the third time at Brentford's Griffin Park ground in West London. I went along as some

sort of deputy snapper with staff photographer Ray Horsnall, while my father was there as the rival paper's sports
editor and he travelled to the game on the Chelmsford team
coach – as sports writers did in those days.

Horsnall and I were forced to drive through London's
rush hour traffic and only arrived at the ground just minutes
before the kick off. As we entered the pitch area, Horsnall
gave me a Rolleiflex camera – he'd given me a rudimentary
lesson on how to focus and click during the car journey -
and sent me off to cover one goal mouth while he went to
focus on the other end.

Within 45 seconds Chelmsford's Bill Cassidy scored what
turned out to be the only goal and, despite being seated on
my camera box for just a few seconds, I swung into action
and managed to point, click and capture Cassidy's post-
goal Alan Shearer-esque raised arm celebration. The picture made it into the paper's sports pages, needless to say
without a credit (again!)

My time at the *Essex Chronicle* was coming to an end as
my three year indenture was almost over. I spent hours
scanning the pages of the *UK Press Gazette*, the important
organ of the media business, in search for new opportunities and I wasn't just interested in jobs in the UK.

Back then there were jobs on English language papers
in places such Kenya, the Bahamas, Hong Kong and Libya
which, for a teenager who had travelled as far as France,
Spain and Jersey, were intoxicatingly exotic and, as it
proved, out of reach. None of my applications were successful – in fact they weren't even acknowledged and I
blame the inefficiency of the international postal service
for this travesty.

Before I did eventually leave – for Kingston (it was Surrey not Jamaica) - the Newsman's old Fashion & Cookery

column changed its title to the marginally less sexist 'Her Page' and we reported that in the light of Harold Wilson's Labour victory in the 1968 General Election, the Chelmsford Arts Festival was to be opened by new Arts Minister Jennie Lee who became probably the most senior Labour politician to visit Chelmsford for decades..

As if to acknowledge my departure to become assistant sports editor on the Surrey Comet, and the fact that things would never be the same again, the Chelmsford Newsman changed its name to the Newsman Herald in February 1968 although it's debatable whether anyone noticed.

And in an edition soon after my departure the paper published a photograph of a retirement presentation to renowned local journalist Gerald Vosper and I was included in the photo along with my father and a host of other local 'scribes.' It was only the second time my picture had appeared in the paper in three years and my post-leaving present was for the caption to credit me with working for the Sussex Comet – so close but no cigar!!

When my granddaughter was about six years old she told us that a photographer from the local paper had turned up at her junior school to snap some summer party shots.

Excitedly she said he was from the "SS Critical" and when we explained that it was called the *Essex Chronicle* and I pointed out that I had worked there for three years as a teenage reporter in the 1960s, she seemed less than impressed and her only response was "why?"

Chapter 14

GOING DOWN 'SARF'

For those of us brought up in God's own country in the Midlands, the so-called great north/south divide was something that went on either side of us and sparked little or no interest. We wallowed in our neutrality like the strawberry jam in the middle of a sponge – a sweet and tasty treat between two layers of plain cake.

However, living in Essex made me a secondary Southerner and one who was blissfully unaware of the other great divide – the two sides separated by the River Thames. From Tottenham to Tilbury and Bow to Brentwood, crossing the river into Kent or Surrey meant going "sarf of the river" and setting foot in the land of the heathen.

Taking a job on the *Surrey Comet* meant that I was guilty of this great sin, of going where a North London cabbie would only go for a triple fare and probably not after dark. But none of this bothered me as I was moving on in my career to be an actual assistant sports editor; a second in command; a deputy sheriff.

My interview was with the paper's editor, a dapper bearded man who, it seemed to me, took everything very seriously. But he was obviously a good judge of character and talent as he offered me the job without too much hesitation – it made me wonder for a moment if I was the only applicant.

Job in hand, I was now on the brink of leaving home at 20 years of age and while Kingston was not Tripoli or Nairobi the whole thing was both scary and overwhelming.

My first days were spent in a dark but probably once imposing three story house where I had a dingy single room with a bed, two chairs, a gas ring and a shared bathroom down the corridor. I had found it through my new 'local' paper before I left Chelmsford and met my Chinese landlord on the day my father drove me to my new life away from the comforts of home.

I soon realised that there were very few comforts of any sort in my new residence but it was a base from whichI could find somewhere more salubrious once I had settled in at the office.

I had no television or record player, just a transistor radio and there was no 'welcome to the doss-house' party with my new house mates.

In fact I never saw any of my 'house-mates' at all and spent that first night walking round Kingston looking for something, anything, that stayed open late on a Sunday. I found a cinema showing an American film about the gangster John Dillinger and it went on until around 10pm – this was my introduction to life in Kingston in February 1968.

In the safety and comfort of my new office, I was seated in a very crowded newsroom opposite my new boss Paul Harrington, a large genial man who welcomed me into the fold with a run-down of the teams, people and places that mattered in and around Kingston. He ranked the very local Kingstonian football team as number one on my list with the teams from nearby Walton & Hersham and Wimbledon close behind.

Somehow he failed to mention the town's history as a Saxon royal borough, that John Galsworthy, the man who wrote *The Forsythe Saga*, had been born there and Jerome K Jerome's famous tale of *Three Men In A Boat* had begun on the river at Kingston. And more importantly he also omitted to tell me that Eric Clapton had been a regular busker on the streets of Kingston-upon-Thames when it had hyphens which, for some reason, were deemed superfluous in 1965. Maybe it coincided with the town being kidnapped and moved into Greater London.

What I knew about Surrey could have been written on the proverbial postcard. I was aware that three Beatles – John. George and Ringo – all had gaffs in the county (two in Weybridge and George in Esher), that the world's richest man J Paul Getty (in 1965) lived at Sutton House near Guildford and that Genesis sort of grew out of Charterhouse School in Godalming. Sadly there didn't seem to be a bus tour of the homes of the "stars of Surrey" but I had enough info to be going on with until four papers (and four years) later I would find myself visiting the homes of two of Surrey's other famous residents - namely Elton John and Pete Townshend.

Luckily one of my new colleagues – a Welshman who was a table tennis wizard despite having a very dodgy leg – knew of a room going in a nice suburban house in a leafy road which was more the sort of Surrey I had in mind when I moved. I jumped at the chance to move on to somewhere more cosy. And it was indeed cosy. The owners lived in the large detached house and had somehow annexed off a bedroom with a small kitchen and bathroom for a suitable tenant and it turned out I was that tenant.

Although I still had no TV and the family record player was still at my parents' house, I did have a radio and more importantly I had a light and airy room where I could lay my head and also a cooker, complete with a gas meter, where I could conjure up a selection of fine dining cuisine … so long as it came in a packet.

Chinese restaurants and Wimpy bars were the locations of choice during my first week of fending for myself coupled with burgers or pies scoffed at the football matches I covered. I did get to enjoy a fine three course dinner – with coffee and liqueurs if you please – when I covered a local football association dinner where Sir Stanley Rous, chairman of FIFA (Fédération Internationale de Football Association), was guest of honour. The meal was much more enjoyable than the speeches although, ever the intrepid reporter, I did grab the head of world football for a quote or two to go with my story.

Kingstonian were an amateur club and among the leading lights in the Isthmian League and they were a joy to cover mainly because their ground was a handy five minute walk from my new home. The club officials made me welcome and the football wasn't bad with Hendon, Enfield and Sutton among the best teams to visit Richmond Road.

Walton & Hersham were about five miles (and a single bus ride) away and competed in the Athenian League alongside the likes of Slough and both Harwich and Harlow from Essex although neither of these places made me feel particularly homesick. Wimbledon's famous Plough Lane ground was about four miles (and another bus ride) in the opposite direction and among their opponents in the Southern League were Cambridge United, Yeovil, Worcester and dear old Chelmsford City who would end the 1968 season as champions.

These were my main stomping grounds and late night football matches meant not having to spend nights in my own company and there were a few social gatherings when the newsroom invited me to drinking, eating and table tennis evenings. They were an amiable bunch with a heavy workload and on most nights we just went our separate ways and mine involved creating exciting meals – if the instructions on the packets were to be believed.

While I had mastered the intricacies of my new cooker when it came to boiling a kettle and also got along with the toaster, there were a whole new set of rules when it came to preparing an actual meal. Vesta meals in a packet were the in-house foods of choice for me in 1968 and they offered up beef curry, chow mein and paella "in only 20 minutes." In fact they were pretty easy to make as you only need a couple of pans – one for the rice and one for the dried powdered sauce which contained the alleged meat content. According to Vesta they were all "a bit different, nice and tasty" - and one out of three wasn't bad as they were certainly "different" in that they didn't bear any real resemblance to the culinary delights of India, China or Spain.

My first attempt at something a la carte was to make a rice pudding. Couldn't be hard I thought – mix rice, milk and sugar together in a bowl and put it all in the oven until hot and bubbling with a crisp brown topping. Then serve with a generous dollop of strawberry jam. All was going OK up to the actual cooking in the oven bit. Apparently there are different sorts of rice – who knew? – and some of them don't like being baked in a very hot oven and they take their revenge by exploding and sticking to the inside of the cooker.

Fortunately the bang wasn't heard by my landlords and two nights of scrubbing with a wire brush removed all trace of the offending mush and at least gave me something to do in the evening.

When I wasn't busy doing sports reporting (or oven cleaning) in the evenings there were regular trips to London to meet with my girl-friend Pat who worked in the City. And when the night was over, she made her way back to Liverpool Street for the journey to Chelmsford and I caught a train from Waterloo back to Kingston. It had a feel of Ray Davies' 'Waterloo Sunset' but with Brian and Pat instead of Terry and Julie.

We had met at Chelmsford's mixed Grammar school in the early sixties but, it has to be said, she was less than impressed by the 'bad boy' image and tendency to truant - I argued that the school hours "didn't suit my lifestyle" which got me more than one detention - and it took some smooth talking to woo her into thinking I was suitable boy-friend material.

It was during one of our romantic London get-togethers that I actually proposed while we were seated in Trafalgar Square – I didn't make it down onto one knee but sat on the side of the famous fountain to pop the question. She said yes and we eventually got formally engaged on May 18 1968, the day West Bromwich Albion beat Everton in the FA Cup Final.

My time in Kingston was short-lived and on one of my trips home (I usually had Sunday and Mondays off) my father asked whether I would be interested in returning to Essex and taking a job at the *Braintree and Witham Times*. To be honest I was grateful for the opportunity to leave Kingston as I found the whole living away from home experience less than exciting.

My editor was, however, less pleased when I told him I was leaving and berated me about letting him down after only three months – I think he called me "ungrateful" = but I didn't really care and I was sort of delighted that my sports editor boss was typically unfazed, although there was part of me that thought he didn't seem to care too much about most things and wasn't going to miss me.

While there was no leaving party or presentation from the paper, I did leave Surrey with a prize that my money certainly couldn't buy. In a Kingstonian FC raffle I won two tickets to the European Cup Final at Wembley which would feature Manchester United against Benfica.

As it took place on May 29 I thought it would make the perfect engagement present for my new fiancée but as it turned out it would be the first of many dubious decisions I would make over the next 50 odd years. For the record others include deciding I could assemble a wardrobe using instructions in Japanese, confusing onion bulbs with daffodil bulbs when it came to planting spring flowers and believing you can cut your own hair in a mirror.

Chapter 15

TIME FOR BRAINDEAD
AND WITLESS

My new job not only meant a return to Essex and the comforts of home where I could call myself a sports editor and also be both the youngest and cheapest in the country. However things would change dramatically when eventually I joined the ranks of the highly-paid professionals and earned the princely sum of £20 a week to be sports editor on the *Braintree & Witham Times* (known locally as the Braindead and Witless).

I was 20 by now and I soon found out that there were drawbacks that went with this new-found fame and fortune as everyone earning over £1000 a year was paid monthly and by cheque. Consequently I was forced, possibly shouting and screaming, to discard all my anti-capitalist beliefs and theories about Government conspiracies and open my first bank account or, in the words of my editor "not get paid." I had sold out to big business and was fast on the way to becoming a fat cat.

The bank I chose back then was Barclays who, famously,

had introduced the country's first credit card in 1966 but, for reasons I didn't understand, didn't offer me one. In fact my new found relationship didn't last long as they got upset about me spending some of my money – and more of theirs – on Christmas presents for family and friends.

When I later moved to join IPC in London I was able to tell them where to put their overdraft as I was now a customer of our very own Queen's bank, Coutts. They had just a handful of branches back then – all in places where the Queen went (which was mainly London and Windsor) - but we IPC employees got a free account with the country's most prestigious bank ... and this meant even better presents for everybody from then on.

I can't say that I knew much about Braintree as it was somewhere I had rarely visited because, according to local rumour, it had little to offer to excite a teenager even though the local works social club was offering an evening's entertainment with what was billed as "2 Recording Groups ... Smoke and the Gonks" but even with an admission price of 5s (25p) plus a 'Coke bar' it was still a night to miss.

Years earlier, however, the town had been listed in the Domesday Book in 1086 as Branchetreu, then lost 865 of its 2300 inhabitants in the Great Plague of 1665 and eventually found fame as a centre for the production of wool and silk which mattered not a jot to me as I was allergic to wool and had never owned anything made of silk ... not even a purse made from a pig's ear.

There were two schools in the town that I had heard of and assumed were named after prominent (dead) people. The John Ray School celebrated a renowned naturalist who was born near Braintree in 1627 and became a Fellow of the Royal Society which, even I knew, was a big thing. The Margaret Tabor School took its name from the local Tabor family who were prominent woollen merchants in the 1500s although Margaret's role in all this remained something of a mystery.

My arrival at the *Braintree and Witham Times* was heralded with a single paragraph at the bottom of a column on page one of the paper in April 1968 which told the town that "Mr Brian Southall has been appointed sports editor." I replaced Johnny Morris (not the one that did animal voices on TV) who was taking on the role of news editor alongside our editor Ken Goodwin, the golf playing swinging bachelor who was in charge of us all.

In addition to these two I think there were around four reporters, a photographer, one sports editor plus a string of contributors who covered everything from motoring, WI meetings and camera clubs. One of the regular features came from Joe Firmin who I think worked for the parent company in Colchester and wrote about farming in his Land At Work column for at least half a dozen papers.

He was a balding man who had a fancy for a pipe and the fact that his photograph appeared alongside his column prompted one of our readers to write with a novel suggestion. Describing Firmin as "a gentleman with a smug expression and a Harold Wilson pipe clamped between his teeth", he asked if we would print instead pictures of some other staff members who, he thought, should "show off their beauty." I wasn't asked to pose for this line-up but he was rewarded with photos of three young ladies – two reporters and the editorial secretary alongside – not instead – of Firmin's pic.

I was in sole charge of the regular three or four pages of sport which involved me writing match reports, sub-editing contributions and designing the page layouts. And everything appeared under a banner which ran across the first page of sport that announced 'Times Sport edited by Brian Southall' and it was in BIG type!

The events I managed to avoid actually going to – which included motor cycling, rugby, bowls, darts, swimming, athletics, cycling, golf, judo and angling – were all covered by a host of enthusiastic supporters who knew their sports backwards but couldn't really write very well.

There was also quoits which was a game I never saw or understood and the scorecards that came in didn't help either – with one side seemingly winning by five heats to three and 22 points – but fortunately there was an expert correspondent on hand to provide a report. The same applied to pétanque which, according to my report, "Hit Braintree with A Bang" when the UK's second pétanque club was formed in a local pub by the man who had started the nation's first club somewhere else and then moved to Braintree to carry on his good work.

I came into the picture when these reports flooded in and once the copy was ready and the pages designed, everything went off to QB the printers in Colchester where, careful to play by the printers' rules I had learnt at the *Essex Chronicle* and not touch anything that wasn't mine, I oversaw the final production process.

QB was a mighty operation in the late 1960s and printed not only the papers owned by the Benham family (the B in printers QB), which included the *Braintree & Witham Times*, *Maldon & Burnham Standard* (known as the Mundane and Boring), *Colchester Gazette* and *Essex County Standard*, but also a host of other titles. One of those was the *New Musical Express* and the fact that they shared print day with us on the *Times* was an opportunity for me to spot the likes of Andy Gray, Derek Johnston, Alan Smith and a young Nick Logan as they gathered together to check stories about The

Beatles, The Stones, Elvis and other assorted stars from the golden decade of pop.

I was tempted to go over and try and sell myself to them in the hope of getting a job – after all I knew how the printers worked, could sub and lay out pages and had an awful lot of pop and rock records. However I curbed my enthusiasm and stuck to the main task in hand which was covering the football teams from Braintree, Witham, Tiptree and Coggeshall.

As all these towns and villages were some miles apart and QB was over 20 miles away, Ken Goodwin saw the need for me to drive and arranged for me to have driving lessons with a local instructor who I insulted on day one. His company name was somebody and son and when my new teacher turned up, bearded and bespectacled, I assumed he was the father and made a throwaway comment about how sharing duties with his son must be good. He then quickly pointed out that his son was just three years old and didn't do much driving and he was going to be the man who would be responsible for teaching me the skills of the road.

Actually we got on pretty well and within about 10 weeks I was ready to take my test which was set for early on a Monday morning after a weekend Pat and I had spent in Paris.

The journey on a Sunday night from Lympne airport in Kent – it had a grass runway - back to Chelmsford in her father's car meant going through south London where we discovered the streets were under a few feet of water from a freak rainstorm.

The journey seemed to take forever and meant I had just a few hours sleep before getting a train to Braintree for my test. I made a point of yawning a lot and when the test man asked if I was OK, I went on (and on) about my night of hell, making our way through the flooded streets of London where people were stranded and hanging out of upstairs windows shouting for help.

I must have painted a vivid picture as the examiner seemed to accept my rather clumsy three point turn and even allowed me a second go at this question. "If the traffic lights are showing just amber what do you on the next light?" Now I knew it had to be stop or go and when I said "go", he looked at me with a raised eyebrow and suggested I have another go. This time I was ready and blurted out "stop". Then he told me I had passed and I thanked my powers of description and the poor rain-sodden people of Lewisham.

Armed with the company's red Ford Escort I was now out and about, here and there but mainly only at weekends. Goodwin nabbed it on weekdays, although I didn't understand why as he had a smart two-seater sports car which fitted perfectly with his image as a ladies' man.

It soon struck me that maybe the examiner might have been a bit too generous in giving me my full licence as, after just a couple of weeks on the road,

I had my first accident. Driving back from Colchester at the end of our press day, I was busy re-tuning the radio to get news of the England football team being picked for their next match when the car in front suddenly stopped. Why? I don't know as I couldn't see any pedestrians, wild boar or wobbly cyclists but it meant I careered into his backside. It was dented bumpers all round with no drivers being harmed in the making of the accident, so it was down to the company's insurance company to sort it out. But having an accident in my first month as a qualified driver did bring it home to me just how dangerous it was out there and that looking where you were going while driving was quite an important rule of the road.

As I didn't always have the company car at my beck, I decided it was time to purchase something of my own and my father – a devoted Renault man - persuaded me to buy a Renault 4 from the local French car dealer (the cars were French not the salesman) in Chelmsford. This turned out to be a massive mistake as the Renault 4 was basically two deck chairs inside a tin box with a strange stick that came at you from the dashboard and had to be pushed in and out to find a gear ... and all that cost a mere £543 when new.

Apparently the bloke who ran Renault had launched it in 1961 as "a family car, a woman's car, a farmer's car or a city car" but it was not the car for a trendy twenty something man about town with people to impress. And the fact was that if you over-choked it on a cold night, it flooded the carburettor (or so I was told) and then the thing would only start (if you were lucky) with the help of an antiquated starting handle. As a way of getting my own back on my father for coming up with the stupid plan to buy the thing, I had no qualms about calling him out on more than one winter's night to collect me from the King's Head Meadow car park in Chelmsford.

On the upside there was never an issue with leaving it overnight in a public car park as nobody in their right mind was going to steal it and in the end I think I just dumped it somewhere and moved on to inherit my father-in-law's mini (which in turn was passed on to my sister-in-law) before entering the jet set with an MG Midget sports car. It was bright red, boasted a top speed of 88mph and could accelerate from 0 to 60mph in just under 20 seconds. I had arrived and was ready to rock 'n' roll on the highways and byways.

In the year I became sports editor Braintree football club took on the name Braintree & Crittall Athletic in an effort to honour their origins as the Crittall Window Company works team. The locally based Crittall company began making metal window frames way back in 1884 and donated the land for the town's football pitch - in return the team were affectionately known as the 'Iron'.

When I joined they were playing in the Metropolitan League which featured the A teams (or third X1s) from the likes of Arsenal, Tottenham and West Ham alongside Bury, Brentwood and neighbouring Chelmsford City's reserve team. Looking through the club's history books I discovered that this was the ninth league they had played in since 1898 – the others included the North Essex League, Mid Essex League, Essex & Suffolk Border League, Spartan League, Eastern Counties League and Greater London League

They had a loyal and long serving secretary named Ron Webb who was a fixture at every game which was fortunate for me as he was more than happy to provide me with a long (sometimes overlong) match report if I was unavoidably unavailable.

The reports were understandably a little biased but none the worse for that, although in 20 years the club had won nothing so there hadn't been much for him to write home about.

The matches against the three teams from the major London First Division clubs featured some youngsters who, and nobody knew back then, would go on to forge careers as professional footballers at the highest level. The goal scorer for an Arsenal A side which drew 1-1 with Braintree was a future England international called Ray Kennedy, while both Steve Perryman and Jimmy Neighbour were scorers for Spurs A when they beat Braintree. Disappointingly I failed to pick any of them out as future stars.

For the match with West Ham A I made the journey (on the team bus) to the London club's Chadwell Heath training ground and as the teams paraded out I thought to myself that it wasn't going to be a day for 'Iron' glory as playing at centre forward for the Hammers was a budding - and huge – 17 year old Bermudian World Cup striker named Clyde Best. He was on his way to a future in the first team but on this day Braintree won 1-0 and I pointed out that Best was "played out of the game by the rugged Braintree defence."

Sadly Braintree won nothing during my tenure as sports editor – indeed they had to apply for re-election to the League after finishing second from bottom – and were, it has to be said, pretty badly supported by the locals. Their less than healthy situation was highlighted when it came to sharing out the receipts from an FA Cup First Qualifying round match at home to Ware in 1967. The attendance was just 243, income totalled £22 9s (£22. 45p) with expenses of £22 3s 6d (£22.17p) which added up to a glorious profit of 5s 6d (27p), which had to be shared with their opponents, leaving Braintree with the princely sum of just 2s 9d (14p) to plough back into the club . If I, or the club, needed re-minding of the perils of surviving in the lower reaches of non-league football then this was it. And to add insult to injury Braintree (or Crittall as they were listed by the FA) lost the match 2-1.

Chapter 16

ONE EYE ON NELSON

On the subject of West Ham footballers, it was always a fascination for us to see who was around and about in Braintree on market day (Wednesdays I think it was) when the local town pubs had extended opening hours. Players whose faces were all too familiar but whose names I will not mention were a regular sight around Braintree and in other local towns on market day as they swept from pub to pub, presumably in an effort to recover from a hard morning's training.

The seemingly ongoing relationship between West Ham and Braintree included their players turning up to support the local Spastics (it was what it was called back then) charity with Johnny Sissons, Brian Dear and Ronnie Boyce all appearing at a six a side football tournament and England World Cup winners Bobby Moore, Geoff Hurst and Martin Peters joining TV stars Leslie Crowther and Simon Dee for a cricket match in aid of the same good cause.

Rumour had it that some of these players also favoured a local restaurant called The Barn run by Bob Patience who, according to local legend, was happy to tolerate some after-hours drinking with the soccer stars. It wasn't the most salubrious place but lived up to its name as a cavernous single space which did actually resemble a barn. There were all sorts of stories about Patience and the people who patronised The Barn – the talk was of the Krays and other London villains - but as far I could see the local paper steered well clear of any investigative reporting, although we did promote appearances by Free and Geno Washington.

In the early 1970s it all fell apart for Patience when he went back to his nearby home to find gunmen threatening to shoot his wife and daughter unless he opened the safe. He hesitated and they shot both of them, killing his wife and injuring his daughter, and made their getaway with a handsome haul of just £90. Some years later two men were convicted of the crimes and jailed.

Being a sports editor was, I quickly discovered, quite an arduous and time-consuming job and one of the things that went by the wayside was pop music. This was something that I had grown up loving as I collected singles and albums by a whole variety of acts including, obviously, The Beatles alongside The Stones, The Who, The Searchers, The Kinks, Ray Charles, Bob Dylan, Joan Baez, Buddy Holly, Them, Billy Fury (my personal rock 'n' roll hero) and Dusty Springfield. There was no room for Cliff Richard or Elvis Presley or those other sixties chart toppers *The Sound of Music*, The Monkees or Val Doonican.

Looking back, and eventually writing books about Beatles' albums, I realised that despite having religiously bought every album from *Please Please Me* to *Sgt. Pepper*, I had missed out on their first ever double album – the eponymous collection *The Beatles*, known to all mankind as *The White Album*.

Being engaged to be married and sort of wedded to my career, buying albums and listening to music had somehow gone out of the window. There was still Radio One which I could listen to in the car (without crashing) and Sunday afternoon's *Pick of the Pops* plus TV's *Top of The Pops* although we had lost *Ready Steady Go!*, *Thank Your Lucky Stars* and *Juke Box Jury*. I was out of it, off the pop radar and not having *The White Album* signified how far I had let my interest in music drift away.

There were no singles on the album so nothing was played on Radio 1 to tease my interest and it became the first Beatles album I didn't buy either on day one or any other day. Somehow I missed it completely and it was almost a decade before I ordered up a free copy from the vaults courtesy of being an employee of EMI.

The Times' modern offices were above a doctor's surgery (in fact my GP's surgery) in a development named Blyth's Meadow, presumably because it used to be a field, Nearby there was a small and very dainty men's boutique and always anxious to dress the part as a modern man about town, I decided to pay a visit. When I happened to mention that part of my lunch hour would be spent in the clothes shop, there were sniggers and chortles and warnings about keeping an eye out for Francis.

Francis was the owner of the boutique, and it also turned out that his surname was Golightly, that he was 'theatrical' and the producer of the local Scouts Gang Show while his mum had a very fancy hat shop next door. Undaunted, I went along to check out the goods and found a pair of trousers that I fancied. Francis, who it has to be said was both charming and as camp as Larry Grayson, ushered me up the stairs to the changing rooms where, behind a skimpy curtain, I began to take my trousers off.

After a few seconds the curtains were flung back and there was Francis eyeing me up and down and asking if everything was alright. I muttered something, pulled the curtains shut, hastily dressed and darted out of the shop saying the trousers were too long. The last thing I heard was Francis shouting "I can sort you out, sir" in a voice that was, unsurprisingly, just like John Inman's in *Are You Being Served.*

Back in the office there were dubious questions mingled with muffled giggles about my lunch time sortie to the clothes shop. They all knew about Francis and while I ignored most of their light hearted but homophobic banter, I joined in by suggesting that Francis must have stood outside the changing room with a mental stopwatch, counted off the seconds as I undid my belt, unzipped my fly and dropped my trousers and then, at the precise moment they were round my ankles, flung open the curtain. It was timed perfectly and showed a master craftsman at work.

Undaunted by the experience, I did venture back to Francis' emporium to buy a raincoat that required no more than a quick fitting over the clothes I had on. I passed over some cash and then, as an added bonus, ran into his mum who was the spitting image of Danny La Rue. It was a very odd experience for a young man who was determined to be a man's man.

There were odd moments when I thought that being a professional wordsmith with, what I considered to be a reasonable creative streak, would make me a perfect fit in the world of advertising and copywriting. What was so special about "Beanz Meanz Heinz" or "Guinness Is Good For You" or even "A Mars A Day Helps You Work Rest And Play." As a consumer (not of Guinness) I could come up with snappy slogans, catchy product names and advertising campaigns for stuff that everybody loved, needed or wanted – even if they didn't know it.

With all this in mind, I sat in my office one afternoon doodling with an idea for a major campaign for a new Ford car which I decided to call the Xplorer (with no E). Even though we were still a few years away from the off-road vehicles and SUVs that would flood the market, my car was one that would go anywhere and take you to new and exciting places in comfort and with confidence.

Having got all this information mapped out on A3 sized sheets of paper - I was happy to leave the actual design of the car to the people at Ford - I sent it off to the UK headquarters of the American car maker ... but alas just like the newspapers in Africa and the Caribbean, I was ignored and my idea presumably tossed in a bin somewhere in Brentwood.

It was a few years before I realised that large companies didn't do their own advertising campaigns but employed huge expensive agencies to do their thinking for them. I would have been better off sending my belter of an idea to one of them.

It was a new lesson learned but I consoled myself that my effort was not entirely in vain as, in 1991, Ford launched a new range of Explorer trucks in America. They used the E but I still think starting with capital X would have been much more Xciting.

Despite having failed to get a reply let alone an interview to my applications for jobs in sunnier climes, I still kept my eye open for new opportunities which might move me along (and up) the journalistic ladder.

That was when Nelson caught my attention and sadly not the cities in Canada or New Zealand although I would have had a go at getting a job in either of those places. The one

on offer to me was in Lancashire where the local *Nelson &
Colne Advertiser* (I think it was called) was advertising for
a sports editor.

I wrote off for an interview without even knowing exactly where it was or what it was but the words Burnley
FC had caught my eye – this was my chance to forget the
Southern, Metropolitan and Isthmian leagues and actually
cover First Division football and sample all the glamour
that went with it.

Burnley was three miles away on the bus from Nelson
and that made it part of the paper's circulation area and
that, like manna from heaven, meant I would be covering
Burnley in 1969 – just seven years after they had lost an
FA Cup Final to Tottenham. They had players like Ralph
Coates, Martin Dobson, Dave Thomas and Andy Lochhead
and finished the 1967-1968 season in 14th place in the
league with a total of 38 points.

In order to pursue my new dream job, I left Chelmsford
at around six in the morning to get to London and then
catch a train from Euston to Manchester. From there it was
cross-country on a stop-start train that took in places I had
only seen in football league tables – Bolton, Blackburn and
Accrington. I finally arrived in Nelson at around lunch time
for my appointment with the editor who was nowhere to
be seen. Had I got the wrong day or was I in the wrong Nelson I wondered?

As it turned out I was in the right place on the right day
and, while I had travelled for around six hours from one
end of the country to the other, the editor only had to come
across the from the nearest pub. He eventually arrived -
late and seemingly half-pissed which I thought was not a
great start.

He then went on to talk over my duties – writing match

reports, subbing copy, laying out pages – and reporting on the day-to-day activities of Burnley FC and then he dropped the bombshell.

We, representatives of the *Nelson & Colne* whatever, were not allowed into the club's Turf Moor ground having earlier been banned by the club chairman Bob Lord (known to some as the Kruschev of Burnley) for some criticism of the team. However, the editor then made it all better by explaining that we were allowed to buy a ticket (on expenses of course) and stand on the terraces to watch the game and report on it.

His consolation prize was to mention that in the summer there was Lancashire League cricket which was regarded by many as being among the finest league competitions in the country and featured many Test cricketers from overseas. He somehow failed to mention that the finest of these West Indian, Australian, Indian and Pakistani players were allowed to play in England's county championship from 1968 and they were now swiftly departing local league cricket like rats off a sinking ship. All this made his eventual offer even less attractive.

I looked on it as a great pity as, to their credit, Nelson had got things rolling back in 1928 when they signed West Indies captain Sir Learie Constantine and paid him £800 a season. Later they followed up with Pakistan's Sadiq Mohammed and Australian Neil Hawke while the fearsome West Indian fast bowling duo of Wes Hall and Charlie Griffith turned out for Burnley and Accrington respectively. But all that excitement was set to slip out of my grasp.

In fact I thought it would take an awful lot to make up for an editor's tardiness, having to report football from the terraces as opposed to a press box – without the delights of tea and biscuits at half time on a wet, cold Saturday afternoon – and cover the leftovers of a once star studded cricket league.

This had been my first trip to the North of England – we have established that Birmingham and Worcestershire are firmly in the Midlands – and it wasn't at all warm and cuddly although I only met one resident in a chilly cobbled back street so it was probably a tad unfair for me to reject it all out of hand. But that was what I did and even before I got back to Essex I had decided to turn down the job that was on offer. It was also one of the more sensible 'Pat-decisions' I made as I know now that she is a lady who could feel chilly without a cardigan in Italy in June.

So, none the worse for my sojourn to the north, it was back to work at the *B&WT* under the watchful eye of the lady who ruled the front desk – and all of us –with a rod of iron. Scottish Anne was not tagged 'Monarch Lord of the Glen' for nothing and she ran a tight ship. She took in copy, booked adverts and notices and made sure everything worked smoothly including the editorial staff who felt duty bound to keep on her right side as the other side could be sharp and cutting.

Having settled back into the routine I took my duties seriously even turning out to present awards at various local sports clubs' annual dinners. I was not exactly billed as a guest of honour but was still expected to make some sort of a speech and not just stand up and hand out the cups and medals. An added task was drawing the raffle and on one memorable night (at the local Shalford football club event) I drew out my own ticket for the top prize. With all the good grace I could muster, I turned it down and pulled out a second ticket – and this time it was Pat's. Now it was an act of God so we took the fruit basket and left.

Back at the printers in my final few weeks at the paper

I met up with my opposite number on the sister *Maldon &
Burnham Times* paper and it turned out that he had been
sports editor at the *Nelson & Colne* newspaper I had applied
to join. I related my tale of the trip to the two towns and the
interview with a late, slightly worse for wear editor who
tried his best to sell me a slightly tarnished job. And when
my new colleague gave his take on life on a paper in Nelson, he ended up convincing both of us that we were well
out of it.

Chapter 17

NO FRIEND OF DOROTHY

Having left two newspapers without any sort of fanfare, leaving party, farewell gift or even a printed acknow-ledgement of my existence, my departure from the *B&W Times* in August 1969 at least warranted a five inch story on page two which included a rather dapper head and shoulders photograph.

I left with something of a heavy heart but London and, even better, Fleet Street beckoned. I was going to work in the very heart of the country's newspaper industry and even though I had been there once before when I was teen-ager, this was a whole new ball game. My new office ad-dress would be 161 Fleet Street, the home of IPC Business Press, a division of Cecil King's vast IPC empire which in-cluded the *Daily Mirror, Sunday Mirror* and *Sunday Pictorial* newspapers.

The offices at 161 were above a Golden Egg restaurant, noted more for its colourful yellow interior (described by one writer as bringing "a jazzy mood to eating in a low-price restaurant") than for its food. IPC was home to a plethora of weekly and monthly publications that could satisfy nearly all the nation's hobbies and interests from cage birds and cycling to football, rugby and music.

Early in 1969 I had applied for a job as a sub editor on the music paper *Melody Maker* and travelled to Fleet Street to meet its legendary editor Jack Hutton and his deputy Alan Walsh. It was an amiable chat and I thought I did rather well, emphasising my all round skills, as writer, sub editor and layout man but it got me nowhere as they gave the job to somebody else.

In what I saw as an effort to placate me, Hutton said he would keep in touch as there were things he had in mind for which I might be just the man and he was as good as his word as he called some months later and invited me back for another interview. And once again Walsh was there but this time in his capacity as editor of a new publication called *Music Business Weekly*.

It was a trade paper aimed at the music business but seemingly all the bits I knew nothing about – retailing, publishing, production, distribution, management and release schedules. The fact that record companies issued records on a Friday and staggered releases so their biggest and best-selling artists didn't clash now made sense to me but as a mere punter, who bought vinyl 'cos I liked it, I had never even thought about who put out what and when.

Publishing was all about the songs and how they had a separate life; being covered by other artists, used in commercials, films or television programmes and all the while earning money – or royalties – for the writers and the song publishing companies. I found out how record shops operated to make sure the records people wanted were in stock and supplied by the record companies' distribution operations, the role of production companies in the creation of music, and what a manager did to earn his 10% - or more in some cases. It was all new to me, but fortunately all I had to do was sub the copy and lay out the pages – the companies, the executives and the numerous behind-the- scenes personalities were as foreign to me as a cake recipe or a car manual.

Walsh, a stocky Scouser with thick Buddy Holly glasses, was my new editor alongside deputy Rodney Burbeck who had worked on a national newspaper (the *Sketch*) and for a record company (CBS). The staffers included industry veteran and publishing expert Nigel Hunter, former *Brighton Argus* reporter and local part-time music promoter Peter Robinson plus Derek Abrahams and our glamourous editorial secretary Christine Rothwell. My immediate boss was chief sub Mike Topp, a fan of the ale who spent a good deal of his free time working night shifts at the nearby *Sun*. I joined this carefully assembled team in August 1969 just a month before I was due to get married and the first edition of *MBW* was set for September 20, a week before my wedding day which did not bode well in terms of honeymoon plans.

On September 27, Pat and I married in the church near Chelmsford where I, my brother and some others who would later fall off the righteous path, were choirboys earning 10s (50p) a month plus half a crown (25p) for weddings. Our honeymoon was spent in London where we saw Ray Charles at the Royal Festival Hall and ate some fancy Italian pasta dishes and zabaglione.

The date we chose was not particularly notable although the month was chosen as there was still some sort of tax allowance for a September wedding and Aston Villa's performance at Portsmouth, where a 0-0 draw left them at the bottom of Division Two, certainly made us the Match of the Day.

Honeymoon over, it was back to work on Tuesday to help produce the second edition of *MBW*. I travelled to London each day by train from Chelmsford into Liverpool Street and then from there it was a bus to the hub of the free press in Fleet Street. We were on the first floor of the office block and looking at the various publications up and down the corridor made it my own little equivalent of Hollywood's Walk of Fame but without the handprints.

Opposite *MBW* was *Melody Maker* with its team of super-star writers – Max Jones, Laurie Henshaw, Ray Coleman, Bob Dawbarn, Bob Houston and Chris Welch – who I had read regularly throughout the sixties. This was the paper and these were the men who informed and influenced me when it came to pop music.

Coleman had toured with The Beatles in 1963 and repor-ted that "If they recorded the national anthem it would top the hit parade" and then, a year later, he hit the road with The Stones and wrote, "Unkempt they (the Stones) maybe but their music has vitality and they are mentally sharp."

He also told everyone, slightly ahead of my own proph-etic words from May 1965 about Bob Dylan, that his single 'The Times They Are A-Changin'' was "a tremendous first single from the folk poet" despite being a record "you can't dance to but you can think about." It was then that I knew me and Coleman were like-minded music fans, although he liked the Carpenters and I didn't, and that was some-thing that we carried through in a friendship that lasted until his death in 1996.

The *MM* had convened something called a 'pop panel' in 1965 to review and decide that The Beatles *Rubber Soul* al-bum was "not their best on first hearing" while mentioning that their final offering *Abbey Road* was "a vast improve-ment on their last album" and was also "the least pretentious set from them in a long while." Various reviewers also mentioned that Cream's *Disraeli Gears* album was "a creation of pure energy", urged people to listen to Pink Floyd's *A Saucerful of Secrets* as "it isn't really so painful" and defined Led Zeppelin's eponymous album as being in "a gas new bag" ... whatever that meant. Still these were all words we devoured avidly, often disagreed with and argued about long into the night.

Next door to *MBW* was *Football Monthly*, the 'bible' of football magazines and further down the corridor was *Disc & Music Echo*, edited at that time by Coleman alongside Penny Valentine and Mike Ledgerwood (who had both appeared on *Juke Box Jury* which made them pretty famous in my eyes), then came *Goal*, the weekly sister publication to *Football Monthly* and then *Rugby World* which I swear was edited by a man called Rupert Bear.

Further along were *Cycling Weekly* and *Bird Cage & Aviary Weekly* and anyone with even the slightest hint of imagination could work out from hair styles, modes of dress and various accoutrements (such as records, bicycles, sports boots or any sort of bird in any sort of cage - gilded or not) who worked where.

However, to Lily (or was it Dolly?) the tea lady we were all the same. Men and women who queued at her trolley for tea or coffee and rolls (cheese or corned beef) and biscuits or cakes for which we handed over pennies rather than shillings. This was my new place of work and it was exciting – I called Ms Valentine by her first name, nodded a hello to Jones, exchanged greetings with Coleman and at one time or another shared the gents with Messrs Welch, Henshaw and Ledgerwood.

We also featured a specialist column on law which was written by a man who was a famous barrister and MP but

appeared under the pseudonym Simon Elliott. There was
another expert who covered classical music. He was a wiry,
petite Australian named Evan Senior who often performed
ballet moves in the office to entertain us and told us that
his claim to fame was being "homosexual, Jewish and a
Freemason." We weren't particularly impressed although
somebody did comment "I didn't know you were a Mason."

Our regular instrument specials came from Chris Hayes
who was actually on the staff of *Melody Maker* but crossed
over the great divide to help us out. Hayes was an extraordinary man who laid claim to being one of the last
people to interview the famous singer Al Bowlly before
he was killed during WWII when a German parachute
mine exploded outside his London flat. Hayes had spent
his whole working life covering music across five decades
having, it turned out, joined *MM* in 1929, three years after
it was launched.

He was a tall, thin man who favoured a trench coat and
trilby and pasted his bus tickets for journeys when on official *MM* duty onto his expenses claims. He also kept his
own obituary up to date and it sat in the paper's files complete with a photograph of him in his Royal Artillery tin
hat.

On the other end of the phone, with his regular columns
from the North, was Jerry Dawson who was based in
Manchester and, on his occasional visits to London, took
great pride in telling us impressionable young whipper-
snappers how the country's last official executioner Albert
Pierepoint was a great friend of his. He also claimed, perhaps humorously, that he had suggested to the notorious
hangman that his retirement pub should be called The Last
Drop Inn instead of The Struggler.

MBW was printed at QB in Colchester so once again I

found myself travelling out to north Essex, this time on a Monday afternoon, to oversee 'putting the paper to bed' or giving it the OK to be printed. With an editorial colleague, I travelled from Liverpool Street to Essex at around lunch time and tried to finish before the last train left for Chelmsford (my stop) and London which we managed to do most weeks. On the odd occasions things didn't go smoothly there were rooms to be had at a local (cheap) hostelry.

Being a sub editor put you firmly at the back of the queue for 'freebies' of any sort. While the writers got to go to both lunchtime and evening receptions, Topp and I were left to get on with subbing and page layouts, while others enjoyed the hospitality of record companies or publishing houses – and they rarely brought back any goodies for the boys stuck in the office.

It was the same story when it came to handing out albums for review; once again Topp and I got the crap – some of it not even worth reviewing. I did for some odd reason get to review the singles for one week only. It was very much a 'Read All About It' moment as I listened intently to every single that came out and decided which should get into the paper's weekly Top 20, Top 50 or Outsiders sections.

Unfortunately it has to be said that I didn't get much right and my big tip for a high chart position was Morecombe and Wise's rendition of 'Bring Me Sunshine' which was a regular in their hugely popular TV show. Did it make it? Did it buggery. But I wasn't the only one with a poor track record for picking the hits. Whoever reviewed the singles in an early edition of BMW nominated 11 singles which would make it into the chart – and only two of them did, so I didn't feel too bad!

For the record those two hits were Des O'Connor's 'Loneliness' (#18) and Marmalade's 'Reflections Of My

Life' (#3), while the likes of Marvin Gaye, Mott The Hoople, Jimi Hendrix plus Bud Flanagan and Tony Blackburn fell by the wayside. There was also the odd single that had no real hope but offered a fascinating view into the future such as Tim Rice and The Webber Group's release 'Come Back Richard, Your Country Needs You' - a song bizarrely about Richard The Lionheart. The reviewer judged it to be a "jaunty up-tempo number" and described them as "talented young writers"

I can't remember if the singles were reviewed on some sort of rotation system but I think Alan Walsh did it a lot in the early days and Peter Robinson certainly took control in later days although I recall that Abrahams had a go for at least one week as it was memorable for a phone call from a disappointed artist.

Abrahams had suggested that a new release by the singer Dorothy (real name Edna) Squires, who had a couple of hits in the late fifties and early sixties, had some merit ..." if you melted it down and made it into a flower pot." Understandably she was not happy and took to telephoning *MBW* to give the writer a piece of her Welsh mind.

Squires, who was banned from the High Court after multiple "frivolous" lawsuits and branded a "vexatious litigant", started by bawling at the IPC switchboard girl who answered her call. Then she was put through to Abrahams and launched into a ferocious rant, littered with obscenities, questioning his right to dismiss her record and demean her singing career. When it was all over, the switchboard lady, who had obviously listened into the conversation, came through to Abrahams to ask if it was 'the' Dorothy Squires. When told it was, she simply said "Well I won't buy any of her bleedin' records". And it seems very few other people did either.

There were also concert reviews and Rodney Burbeck
came back from a Cliff Richard show at the Finsbury As-
toria (before it became the much hipper Rainbow) to sur-
mise that the singer's original fans from a decade earlier
"must be wedded to fish fingers and nappies by now." He
also pointed out Richard talked at some length about Chris-
tianity and also sang his (Cliff's that is) favourite song from
The Sound of Music but failed to mention what it was.

MBW was launched in competition to the established
music trade paper *Record Retailer* which had first appeared
in 1959 and was established as the home of the 'official'
UK charts. It was stiff competition for us 'newbies' but we
did our best with an unbeatable offer for readers to travel
to Cannes in the South of France for the annual music industry event named Midem.

Anyone in the music business could register and attend
the week long round of meetings, lunches and dinners
and courtesy of *MBW* they could have a room in a ** star
hotel for seven nights for £55.3s (£55.15p) while a stay at
the de-luxe Carlton would run out at £75.5s (£75.25p). This
covered air fares and transfers, but you had to find someone
to share with and you only got a croissant for breakfast.

In an effort to attract readers the paper also ran a small
classified adverts column which featured ads from deal-
ers offering deleted and current records and insurance
companies covering musicians' vans and instruments The
situations vacant section offered people the chance to get
into 'showbiz' – perhaps starting out as a salesman (never
a saleswoman) for an instrument showroom with "prefer-
ence being given to applicants who play the violin."

I did get to see some shows during my time with *MBW*
courtesy of record company tickets including the Incred-
ible String Band at the Royal Festival Hall and either Tim

When tickets went on sale, I queued to pay out the princely sum of £3 for two tickets to see The Who perform their rock opera *Tommy* at the London Coliseum in December 1969. The show was filmed, with co-managers Kit Lambert and Chris Stamp as directors, and a DVD was eventually released in 2009 - forty years later.

Rose or Tim Buckley or Tim Hardin – American folk singers called Tim confused me. One show that I do remember (and not just because it wasn't a freebie) was The Who performing *Tommy* at the London Coliseum in December 1969. I went to the theatre from Fleet Street in my lunch hour and bought a pair of tickets (prices ranged from 30s (£1.50p) down to 10s (50p) and I count myself and Pat among the 2000 fans who were privileged to see the rock opera performed in London's largest theatre which was also home to Sadlers Wells Opera Company.

Jack Hutton was determined to make us lot at *MBW* feel part of his music empire (which also included *Disc*) and in late 1969, just after we had been launched, we were invited to the *MM* Awards ceremony being held in the fancy Waldorf Hotel. 'Do's' in fancy five star London hotels were not an everyday experience for me and certainly a pop music awards event was a brand new experience which I savoured from a suitable distance.

Who was there? It's hard to say except that Christine Perfect, voted top female artist, was there, with her husband John McVie, and maybe some other Fleetwood Macs. Christine was in one of the shortest skirts I had ever encountered, which I admired but this time from an appropriate distance.

One of Britain's emerging musical movements in the early 1970s was 'pub rock' which centred around bands who played on the country's burgeoning pub circuit. There was Dr Feelgood, Kilburn and The High Roads and Brinsley Schwarz who were actually named after a man of that name. This was when I first saw how far the record business could and would go in terms of extraordinary and bizarre promotional ideas. But sadly I didn't see it at first hand as Burbeck wangled it so that he was our man on the plane.

The band's manager Dave Robinson, who later helped found Stiff Records (where they came up with the famous t-shirt slogan 'If It Ain't Stiff It Ain't Worth A F***'), had a scheme to take a bunch of journalists to New York to see the band play at the Fillmore East in April 1970. While the band were delayed on their journey to America – they had to enter via Canada in a light aircraft – the journalists, plus a bunch of *MM* competition winners, were also held up.

During a four hour wait, the scribes, not surprisingly, took to drink (there was a free bar) and eventually arrived in New York either drunk or hungover (or in some cases both). To make matters worse the show was not great, the band got pretty poor reviews and the whole event eventually went down in rock 'n' roll history as the 'Brinsley Schwarz Hype.' There was a rumour that the band didn't even know journalists were being brought out for the show and, according to Burbeck the whole thing was a PR disaster and cost somebody – the band, their manager or their record company – a lot of money and earned nobody any brownie points.

While we subs were not at the front of the queue when it came getting any perks or freebies, we did get to see and meet some of the industry's leading PR people as they wandered from *Disc* to *MM* to *MBW* – once you got past the front desk it was a publicist's dream having the cream of Britain's music writers not just under one roof but within 50 yards of each other. The likes of Stan Britt (A&M), Lon Goddard (CBS), Brian Gibson (Pye) and the never to be forgotten or forgiven Max Clifford whose PR company looked after the likes of Paul and Barry Ryan and Joe Cocker.

Clifford was outwardly charming and once gave me a free copy of Cocker's *Mad Dogs And Englishmen* for no other reason than I was a fan. However, even back then, there was a sleazy side to him, which included open house offers to pornographic film shows in flats around London which were presumably unoccupied as the instruction was often "bring your own chair." In the best traditions of journalists I made my excuses and didn't go but all this dubious activity gave rise to Clifford being known throughout the business as "The Blue Max."

Chapter 18

GOING FOR GOAL

It seemed appropriate, during the latter part of the 1969-1970 football season, for me to get a transfer (for no money at all) to *Goal*. I was frustrated with some of the stuff that was going on at *MBW* and decided that a move along the corridor to the front of the building and into an office overlooking Fleet Street would be a good idea.

In common with all the other offices, *Goal* followed the IPC management's principle of crowding their teams of creative people into the smallest space possible. Each publication along 'my' corridor was invariably housed in one office with the editor maybe having a separate space in a corner somewhere. *Melody Maker* seemed to be the exception as Jack Hutton had somehow wangled himself an actual office next door to his staff.

At *Goal* the editor was Alan Hughes, a respected Fleet Street man who worked for the *Daily Mail* and *Daily Sketch* before helping to launch *Goal* in 1968 as a weekly magazine to run alongside the long-established *Football Monthly*. I was joining as a writer – no more subbing or layouts or late nights at the printer – although we didn't actually go to games and do match reports. The magazine was feature based, although results and league tables and a host of statistics were created by our resident 'stats supremo' Pikey - who these days would qualify as a 'nerd' but was actually a fascinating fount of knowledge. There were, I think, four of us who qualified as the writers with Ray Bradley, a smart, usually be-suited veteran of the 'Street' with a journalist's paunch, undoubtedly the top dog. A slightly built Scotsman, Fulton Geddis, who was the perfect illustration of the word 'wee', was in charge of all the design and page lay-outs.

I think he had a good knowledge of football but this could be overridden by his love of a good picture. It didn't matter how good or bad the player was, if we had a great action photo then one of us was despatched to produce a few hundred words about that player, often with the help of a team mate or manager.

I got my call to duty on Graham Cross, a Leicester City player who ranked some way below Paul Madeley of Leeds and England, when it came to versatile footballers despite making a record 599 appearances for his home town club. He played in positions that were back then called inside forward, centre half and right half and when I rang the club's manager Frank O'Farrell to get some information to go with the photo, he was pretty effusive in his praise for Cross.

However when the piece appeared there were letters from Leicester supporters telling me that Cross was not a lot of cop, was a lucky b*****d and that O'Farrell only said nice things because he had to justify paying his wages. It was harsh but the fans had a right to be heard as well.

European football was covered for the magazine by an exotic character named Leslie Vernon who it was rumoured had escaped from Hungary during the 1956 revolution.

LP LONGACRE PRESS LIMITED

161/166 FLEET STREET LONDON EC4   Telephone 01-353 5011

Mr. Brian Southall,
74B Baddow Road,
Chelmsford,
Essex.   15th April, 1970.

Dear Mr. Southall,

We have pleasure in confirming your transfer from Music Business Weekly to Goal at a salary of £1,768. 0. 0. per annum.

The appointment will commence on the 27th April 1970 and may be terminated by either party giving to the other three month's notice in writing. All other terms and conditions of your employment remain as set out in our letter of the 31st July 1969.

If you agree that this letter correctly sets out the terms of your transfer, would you please sign and return the attached copy to me.

We take this opportunity of wishing you every success in your new appointment.

Yours sincerely,

V.J. Green,
Personnel Manager.

CHARLES BUCHAN'S FOOTBALL MONTHLY · GOAL · CYCLING & SPORTING CYCLIST · DISC & MUSIC ECHO · KINE WEEKLY KINE & TV YEAR BOOK · MELODY MAKER · MELODY MAKER YEAR BOOK · RUGBY WORLD · SPORTING RECORD · SOCCER GIFT BOOK · FOOTBALL STAR PARADE

A MEMBER OF THE ILIFFE-NTP INTERNATIONAL GROUP

It was a transfer but not as we know them. My move to *Goal* from *Music Business Weekly* took place in April 1970 and involved an annual salary of nearly £1,800 which was almost a mighty £600 above the average UK wage

It was during the time when the USSR had been invaded. He was bearded, favoured a big coat and a winter hat and said very little when he delivered his copy. What was his real name, could he have been a spy or a great resistance fighter? We never found out anything more than that he had seen Ferenc Puskas, the greatest Hungarian footballer of all time, play and that was enough for us.

There were days when we had famous visitors to the office. Bobby Charlton, when Manchester United were in town, would occasionally pop along and say hello to Alan Hughes and no doubt discuss the great footballer's weekly column which was probably written by the editor. Bradley was a Londoner and seemed to be mates with Bobby Moore and Geoff Hurst and they occasionally came in after a lunchtime get together. No matter how famous they were, we knew it was not cool to ask these stars for their autographs so we kept our distance.

Hughes was a Brummie and we had many a friendly chat about the merits of his beloved Birmingham City team and my favourites Aston Villa. He was impressed that Gerry Hitchens was a family friend and liked the idea of me doing a piece on his time playing in Italy. He had signed for Inter Milan in 1961, moved on to Torino and Atalanta before ending his 'continental' career with Cagliari in 1969.

Most of the interviews were done on the phone – nobody ever went to a training ground or a player's home (it was cheaper to use the phone) – and I called Hitchens at his home in Wales for our chat. He spoke happily about playing in Italy and for England and about the few other British players in Serie A back then; Denis Law, Jimmy Greaves, Joe Baker and John Charles.

Off the record he pointed out the difference in training methods and some of the things players were taught in order to get through a game in Italy in the sixties. Defenders were encouraged to pick up dirt and throw it into the eyes of attackers at corners and to grab an opponent's most delicate parts as they jumped for a cross. And then there was the trick of going to help an opposition player to his feet after a tackle and either standing on a foot or grabbing and squeezing the inside of an arm at the same time in the hope of getting a violent reaction and maybe a sending off. These were dark arts performed in Italy but I wasn't sure I would get away with any of them in my local Sunday League ... and if I did I would probably get a thumping in the car park afterwards.

My hero Gerry Hitchens appeared on the cover of *Football Monthly*, a magazine I read as a youngster. I ended up writing for its sister publication *Goal* where, in an in-depth interview, Hitchens gave me the low down on Italian dirty tricks

Bryan King had been a team mate of mine in local football before he moved on to join Millwall in 1967 so it made sense for me to interview him for *Goal*. Again we chatted over the phone and King, who, like all goalkeepers, had enormous hands, invited me along to a game at The Den to see him in action. It was also a chance to reminisce about the days when he was our last line of defence and I was an underrated midfield dynamo.

The Den in 'sarf' London was an intimidating place with fans who had a formidable reputation for violence and fences had been erected around the pitch area in the sixties. Despite this I decided to watch the game from the terraces even though King had left me tickets for the stand, and enjoyed, as a neutral, the banter from the home crowd.

The unforgettable moment came when former Spurs player Keith Weller fed a wonderful defence-splitting pass through to Derek Possee who thumped the ball into the net.

It brought great joy and delight to the Millwall fans who erupted in a bout of cheering and chanting of the names Weller and Possee. When it all died down, one supporter, a huge man wearing a well-worn flat cap, turned to his mates and uttered the immortal line, "That Weller, he could f*** my old lady." Surely no greater praise would ever come the way of the former Spurs player as his career progressed to take in Chelsea, Leicester and England.

My greatest claim to fame at *Goal* came with the phrase "I covered the 1970 World Cup" – and I did but in an office in Fleet Street. Editor Alan Hughes was our man on the spot in Mexico while we staffers took down his copy whenever he phoned in from Guadalajara or, just once, Leon, after England's games. The telephone lines from Mexico weren't bad and we got regular news from Hughes for each week's issue during England's campaign up to the quarter finals.

As the new football season started in August 1970 I was sent to the Great Northern Hotel across London on a Friday to write what was to be a 'colour' piece about Manchester United and their new manager Wilf McGuinness who had replaced the legendary Sir Matt Busby the previous season. Under his leadership the team had finished 8th and were now looking for an improvement utilising the skills of George Best, Bobby Charlton, Pat Crerand, Denis Law and Brian Kidd.

It seems the team's only visit to the capital that month was to Arsenal but my best recollection is of settling into an armchair in the hotel and chatting briefly to McGuiness who was charming and enthusiastic. As I looked around I then saw the likes of Charlton and Law and Crerand enjoying afternoon tea and noticed that there was no sign of the great George Best. One of the players I spoke with said nobody had seen him since they'd arrived and didn't expect to catch sight of him until the team left for Highbury the next day. The fact that they lost 4-0 (with Best) didn't help McGuinness' cause and he was replaced, albeit temporarily, by Busby four months later.

Goal was an enjoyable few months covering football at the highest level but it made me realise, even back then, that in many ways the 'beautiful game' was all about money. There weren't any real agents so it was left to the players to get whatever they could and this included often asking for a fee to talk to the press. Our policy was not to pay for interviews but it wasn't always easy having to explain that you couldn't throw £25 or £30 quid into the player's pool.

Chapter 19

YOU'D THINK THE RUSSIANS WERE AT CROYDON

With the World Cup over and the 1970 season underway I asked for a transfer back down the corridor and
was allowed to leave *Goal* for an undisclosed fee (nothing!)
to return to *MBW* where I was anointed as chief sub-editor
under the editorship of Rodney Burbeck who had replaced
Alan Walsh some time during my absence. Nothing much
had changed and most of the staff were the same but things
took a turn for the worse near the end of 1970.

Jack Hutton, who was instrumental in launching *MBW*,
decided to vacate his role as editor of *Melody Maker* in
order to start a new music paper called *Sounds*. The first
edition appeared in October and Hutton recruited a number of ex-*Disc* and *MM* people including Penny Valentine,
Billy Walker and Roy Eldridge along with some of the advertising hierarchy. The powers that be at IPC were less
than pleased with Hutton's move and somehow contrived
to take it out on us at *MBW* in an act of what we saw as

petty revenge. They came up with financial forecasts for the paper's future advertising revenue which were plainly unachievable in a business which was struggling to support two trade publications. Within weeks we were shut down and P45s were handed out and received like invitations to a not so favourite maiden aunt's birthday party.

For some unknown reason, however, I was kept on – the only one of the *MBW* staff to stay with IPC - and late in 1970 I was offered the job I had applied for back in early 1969; sub editor on *Melody Maker*. Having spent my early years as a journalist with no further ambition than to maybe one day work for either (or both) *Football Monthly* and *Melody Maker*, I was now about to achieve my goal – albeit working for *Goal* and then *MM* and doing both without leaving the building.

I was now a fully paid-up member of the *MM* club and nobody could take that away from me. My name was in the editorial box – usually printed on page four with all the pop news – and eventually I moved up from last place on the list when fellow sub Geoff Brown joined and went to the bottom of the line-up.

My new editor was to be Ray Coleman, a fastidious man who was prone to washing his hands a hundred times (alright maybe 20 or 30) a day and even changing his shirt. He was also an *MM* legend having joined in 1960 and worked throughout the sixties beat boom before departing to edit *Disc* in 1967. With Hutton's departure he was brought back to run *MM* and he relished his return to the paper that was his first love; it was said that he had even named his two sons Mark and Miles in tribute to the paper.

This was a time of change for MM and not just because Hutton had left and taken a few writers and subs with him to *Sounds*. Stalwarts of the paper like Bob Dawbarn and Bob

Some years after the closure of *Music Business Weekly* a random
selection of old staff members met up in Abbey Road Studios at
some music event and posed for a reunion photo. Editorial secretary
Christine Eldridge is surrounded by (l to r) Peter Robinson, Rodney
Burbeck, Brian Southall and Nigel Hunter

Houston also decided to leave and a team of young blades
was recruited from local newspapers around the country.
Richard Williams came from Nottingham, Roy Hollingsworth from Derby, Chris Charlesworth from Bradford and
Mick Watts from Walsall and they all embarked on new careers covering the finest in contemporary music.

While there were no assigned areas of expertise, this new
MM editorial team were either experts on or simply fans of
certain artists. I recall that deputy editor Williams was into
Roxy Music, Captain Beefheart, John Lennon, The Beach
Boys and The Band while news editor Charlesworth went

with acts like The Who, Slade, Alice Cooper and Black Sabbath.

Watts, on the other hand, favoured the likes of Randy Newman, Syd Barrett, Iggy Pop, The Stones and David Bowie, who actually attributed his renaissance in the early seventies to Watts and *MM*. In a January 1972 interview Bowie admitted being gay and in the article Watts wrote "David's present image is to come on like a swishy queen, a gorgeously effeminate boy. He's as camp as a row of tents with his limp hand and trolling vocabulary." The feature appeared under the headline "Oh You Pretty Thing" and it was all pretty strong stuff for 1972. Bowie was seemingly unconcerned about it and even confirmed later, "It was *Melody Maker* that made me."

Meanwhile, features editor Chris Welch covered the likes of Yes, Cream and Genesis in addition to his regular witty (occasionally cutting) reviews of the week's singles, while Hollingsworth took care of Leonard Cohen, The Byrds, Marc Bolan and Rod Stewart, although none of this was ever cast in stone. What was certain, however, was that Max Jones, a bald-headed man who wore a beret at almost all times, would focus on jazz.

He had joined *MM* in 1944 and had interviewed and reviewed all the jazz greats over more than three decades including Louis Armstrong who, he told us with great glee, had a great fascination for toilets, visiting them when and wherever possible and boasted of using one in the Pope's enclave in the Vatican. Alongside Jones in the paper's veterans' corner was Laurie Henshaw who focused on gathering news and covering MOR (middle of the road) acts such as Frank Sinatra, Dean Martin and even Cliff Richard.

My place among this collection of wordsmiths was on the subs desk alongside chief sub Alan Lewis. We sat opposite each other at one end of a set of six desks pushed together to accommodate Williams, Watts, Hollingsworth with space for another sub. This was, after all, a paper producing 148-page editions which sold over 200,000 copies a week, making it the biggest and the best music publication in the world ... and I was part of it.

I had grown up with *MM*, alongside *NME*, throughout my school days and was now in a position where I got an official free copy (I had surreptitiously nicked one ever since walking into IPC in 1969). And amongst its most legendary features was the small ads section where musicians advertised to meet like-minded artists or to find a band on the lookout for a bass player or drummer. Pop music history shows us that any of those out of work musos who had a van and a driving licence stood the best chance of being hired.

Without a small ad in *MM*, Noel Redding would probably never have joined Jimi Hendrix in the Experience, Bill Bruford might never have recruited Jon Anderson and Chris Squire into Yes and Genesis would never have found Steve Hackett ... it was truly the musician's paper.

The *MM* office, compared with *MBW* and Goal, was a cavernous space which was home to well over a dozen people with an office manager and his assistant joining the editorial staff. They were in charge of maintaining the copious number of photographs *MM* had collected over the years which were stored in banks of filing cabinets. This was also the charts department where *MM*'s albums and, more importantly back then, singles charts were compiled from a combination of phone calls to retailers and postal returns.

It wasn't rocket science and lacked the accuracy of later official UK charts but it was a pretty good guide to the nation's best sellers, although there were stories of 'chart fix-

ing' back in the sixties. On one occasion a record producer
apparently rang *MM* and offered money to the compilers
for his record to go into the chart in a particular place inside the Top 20 – not too high he thought or that would
arouse suspicion. I never did find out whether any money
changed hands but the record in question actually went
straight into the Top Ten of its own accord.

Subbing and designing pages was one of the least glamorous tasks on the paper, appreciated only by your colleagues. It involved taking the copy from a writer, reading
it through to check the grammar, spelling and for any obvious mistakes and then designing the page it was assigned
to. Now my nemesis in all this, and had been for some time,
was casting off which was estimating, once you'd decided
on the column width and type size, how long the feature
would run for.

As subs we were supposed to know how long a typed
800-word feature would run for in either 8 point or 9 point
type and it was a skill that I never seemed able to master.
One way was to get a copy of a previous edition, find a feature, work out how many lines of printed copy added up
to 100 words and then do a word count of the feature you
were subbing. For instance if 100 words of printed copy set
in 9 point type across a 10 ems column measured around
two inches you had an idea that a 800 word feature would
run to 16 inches – then you could design the page around
the words and add a picture of an appropriate size.

Where could it go wrong I ask myself even now? I have
no idea whether it was my measuring or counting or multi-
plication that was at fault. As often as not I was always long
– sometimes copy running over 6 inches too long for the
page – and then it was case of quietly cropping the photo
or chopping the text in the hope that nobody would notice.

If they did, no one ever mentioned my lack of expertise in this area – maybe I had other skills that made up for it such as coming up with clever headlines that could be puns, a play on a song title, a well-worn phrase or a quote from the article.

Disappointingly, 50 years on I can't remember a single headline that I created to go with a feature in *MM* which might be a comment on the sort of stuff I came up with, but credit where credit's due, I think it was Alan Lewis who, on the death of a blues legend, came up with the headline "Didn't wake up this morning." Genius.

It helped us subs if there was a routine and ours involved getting rid of things like album review pages or left-over features early in a new week and also sorting out the page of readers' letters. These letters came in from fans wanting to know how artists produced certain sounds, which guitar strings or drumsticks they favoured and the merits of the plethora of amplifiers on sale.

These letters were handed over to Chris Hayes who was meticulous in his research to find answers to these enquiries. He was also unfazed by talking to pop stars. After getting a phone number for maybe Eric Clapton or Robert Plant or Rod Stewart from one of his 'younger' colleagues – and this was a day when music reporters did have artists' home phone numbers – he would innocently ring them up.

To his further credit Hayes was never fazed by the fame of the people he called, always introducing himself with the line "Hello Chris Hayes here, *Melody Maker*'s readers' letters column. I wonder if you can help me." And invariably they did, giving Hayes a sensible and helpful answer.

One of my regrets is that I never actually wrote a feature for *MM*; after all with the team of writers they had on call who needed me to interview anybody? In fact the only

writing I ever did was as an emergency album reviewer
when, at the printers, we fell short of copy and had to find
something to fill a page. I went to QB (*MM* was printed there
as well) with Laurie Henshaw and we usually had with us
a few nondescript albums that we could review without
hearing them in order to find the 40 or 50 lines needed to
fill a column.

We had stock phrases we could use for these throwaway
albums which were usually collections by MOR or country
artists. There was always "A fine collection of songs that
will be loved by regular fans" or "for those who like this
sort of music, this is a fine collection of tracks." It was harsh
but needs must when there was a two or three inch gap to
be filled.

Laurie Henshaw was an extraordinary character who
travelled from Brighton every day and had regular anec-
dotes about who was on the train – Laurence Olivier, An-
nie Nightingale or Flora Robson – and a store of great say-
ings that he called on when appropriate. "It's hotter than a
hampton on a honeymoon" was one for a warm summer's
day, alongside "He got the biggest shock since Ruth Snyder"
(I had to look that one up to discover that Snyder was elec-
trocuted in US in 1928 for murder). However, my personal
favourite was, "He moved so fast you'd think the Russians
were at Croydon." You had to be there to understand the
reference to the threat posed by the USSR behind the Iron
Curtain back in the 1960s.

While Henshaw (and Hayes) came from Brighton and
Coleman commuted in from Shepperton, I travelled in on
the train from Chelmsford to London and it was fortunate
that *MM* (like *MBW* and *Goal*) didn't have any set office
hours. You worked a full day and were expected to start
somewhere around 9.30am or 10am but there was no sign-

ing in or clocking on so being a bit late was OK. And if there had been a late night at the printers I would occasionally have a day off midweek, usually Wednesday.

Pat and I had moved from our first home together – a flat rented to us by a Chelmsford City footballer pal of my father who had given us first dibs without an interview or any references – to our first house in the village of Cressing near Braintree, about 11 miles from Chelmsford. The three bedroomed semi-detached house cost just over £4000 and was the start of my daily two hour journey to work by car, train and bus which seemed more 'Semi-Detached Suburban Mr James' (Manfred Mann 1966) than 'Rock'n'Roll Hero' (Meat Loaf 1986).

I realised soon after joining that there were real and obvious benefits to being on the staff of the country's leading music paper. You could ring most record company press offices and blag an album (EMI was always the most difficult, something I tried to change later in the seventies) although concert tickets were harder to get hold of. And then there was the dress code.

Of course there wasn't one at MM. In fact there hadn't been one at either *MBW* or *Goal* (although very long hair was frowned on despite George Best's 'Beatle' cut) but MM was a fashion free-for-all with the bad taste of the seventies to the fore. Shoulder length hair, loon pants, tank tops and wide-collared flowery shirts were all part of the 'uniform' alongside some of the weirdest boots you could imagine including stack-heeled platforms. While these made you at least three inches taller, they left you in danger of breaking a heel when getting off a bus in Fleet Street and having to limp off to find a heel bar. It was a sad and embarrassing experience for any red-blooded male to go through.

We were quite a long way from the heart of London's

fashion industry in the West End and our end of town boasted very few up-to-date clothes shops let alone anything that resembled a boutique. National newspaper journalists were not noted for their fashion sense and the legal profession was all about suits and waistcoats when they weren't parading about in wigs and gowns.

The nearest fashionable menswear shop was a branch of Take Six which sat in Ludgate Circus, at the end of Fleet Street on the way up to St Pauls Cathedral and it was an oasis in a desert of grey and black worsted or brown tweed. They had fancy flowered shirts, wide bottomed trousers in crushed velvet and zip-up suede jackets in a range of outrageous colours. A week didn't go by without somebody on the paper buying something that they thought was the pick of seventies gear.

Proof of the fashion sense of *MM*'s editorial team was there for all – well all IPC employees and their families – to see when the company in-house newspaper IPC News came along to an *MM* editorial meeting in August 1971 with a cameraman. The photos showed an excess of hair, people wearing dark glasses during the day plus smoking in the office. The feature, on what was described as the company's "complete music paper for the thinking fan," concluded that the meeting was "intellectual, arrogant, genial, calm and productive." What did they expect – lines of drugs, bottles of booze and loud music?

However, what Fleet Street lacked in fashion outlets, it more than made up for in pubs and wine bars which could be found in the plethora of alleyways and side streets that branched off the home to half a dozen of the country's national newspapers.

For centuries the profession of writing had been synonymous with heavy drinking and not for nothing did

Private Eye come up with the name 'Lunchtime O'Booze' as their archetypal hack.

Oddly neither *MM* nor *MBW* (although *Goal* was a different matter altogether when it came to lunchtime drinking) had any serious boozy writers. Certainly the new young bloods were too professional to get distracted by drinking sessions - although going out to see certain artists did involve a certain amount of social imbibing - and there were no obvious signs of any drug taking which was something Coleman would not have allowed.

However, there was one pub that was frequented by staff on *MBW*, *MM* and *Disc* – plus some advertising people from a nearby agency who we made a point of ignoring – and that was the Red Lion in Red Lion Court, one of the many alleys that led off Fleet Street. It had opened in 1571, survived the Great Fire of London and its cramped homely atmosphere (and location next to the offices) made it the handiest hostelry. It was owned and run by Wally, a rotund camp gentleman who favoured a cravat at all times.

In addition to its small ground floor bar area there was a slightly bigger restaurant on the first floor which served a selection of English and Oriental food – steak and chips sat alongside a selection of Thai curries and Chinese dishes – and it was here where you could spot the occasional celeb. Some of the people who wandered down to London EC4 to do an interview with *MBW*, *MM* or *Disc* would often end up in Wally's dining room – and to get there they had to go through the bar.

It was there, as I sipped orange juice (although I had developed a taste for champagne after my wedding), that I spotted Joe Cocker and Ray Davies plus Radio 1 DJs John Peel and Stuart Henry. Across the road from Red Lion Court, in Fleet Street, was the legendary El Vino's wine bar which I had heard of but, by 1971, had never actually set foot inside. This was partly due to the fact that I did not drink wine but had more to do with me not knowing anyone who would take me in there.

It was the home of proper Fleet Street journalists and boozers, who stood (or leant) alongside members of the legal profession whose chambers were strung along Fleet Street. It was also frequented by the higher ranks of music business PRs such as Leslie Perrin (The Rolling Stones), Tony Barrow (The Kinks, Andy Williams, The Monkees) and Derek Taylor (Apple and The Beatles) when they came a-calling.

Back then I never got to meet any of them but as the years passed I would have dealings with all three including collecting the Les Perrin PR Award from his widow for the work done by my EMI press office team in the 1980s. And where is the award now we ask? Certainly not in my trophy cabinet – although there would be plenty of room – and probably not with what is left of EMI after three office moves and two takeovers.

In early 1972, before I left *MM*, there was a splendid, almost no-expense-spared affair at the famous Wig & Pen Club in Fleet Street, near my favourite cigar shop, when Ray Coleman celebrated with his staff the fact that *MM* had earlier passed the 200,000 sales mark. So after working on well over 70 editions of the most famous music paper in the world, it was time to move on (again) and this time it was back along the corridor to *Disc* for my fourth move in as many years – and still no money had changed hands.

Chapter 20

IS THAT JIMMY PAGE
I SEE BEFORE ME?

O ddly, *Disc* was not a music paper I ever bought or even read. It was far too pop orientated for my eclectic taste in music which ran towards the likes of Van Morrison, Stevie Wonder, Al Green, Randy Newman, Harry Nilsson, The Byrds and John Lennon rather than The Osmonds, David Cassidy or The New Seekers.

But persuaded that, while I was predominantly to be chief sub, there would be opportunities for me to put pen to paper, I climbed aboard the good ship *Disc & Music Echo* to give its full title back then. In fact it had started out as simply *Disc* in 1958, taken over *Music Echo* in 1966 and adopted the full name before reverting back to *Disc* just after I joined. By that time you could get your weekly fix of *Disc* for just 6p which was 1p cheaper than *Melody Maker* but I think a good deal thinner.

Succeeding Coleman as editor was a short rotund occasionally red-faced Scotsman called Gavin Petrie, now a famous comedy script writer along with his wife Jan Etherington. He had a penchant for loud plaid trousers - not exactly traditional Highland dress as they were flared hipsters.

The established crew back then was assistant editor David Hughes, features editor Caroline Boucher and news editor Mike Ledgerwood who, in addition to an incredibly fast sprinter's walk and the shiniest shoes I had ever seen, always reminded me of Buffalo Bill with his swept back curls.

Disc editorial staff line-up for a team photo in 1972 at the joint leaving party for Phil Symes and David Hughes (l to r front row kneeling) alongside Bill Kellow. The rest of the team (minus editor Gavin Petrie) in the back row are (l to r) Rosalind Russell, Caroline Boucher, Brian Southall, Mike Ledgerwood, Judy Noakes and Jack Oliver

Other writers included soul aficionado Phil Symes, Rosalind Russell and, a little later, Andrew Tyler. We were all housed in one office with Petrie and his secretary portioned off in a separate glass walled executive retreat.

They were a genial bunch and, to be fair, *Disc* had established itself as a leading light in the equality stakes by giving women a fair chance in the male-dominated world of newspapers. Penny Valentine had cut her teeth with the paper in 1964 and was followed by Boucher and Russell – which was three more ladies than *MM* or *NME* could boast in an editorial capacity.

While it sailed a long way behind *MM* and *NME* in terms of sales figures, *Disc* led the way in its use of colour on both the front page and the weekly pull-out pop poster which also included occasional sports stars such Andre Agassi and Bjorn Borg. The poster photo came from a range of music industry photographers including Mick Rock, his then-wife Sheila Rock, Barry Plummer and Mike Putland who was the most regular and took on the role of *Disc*'s go-to snapper, accompanying writers on feature assignments.

We also had our own exclusive cartoonist in Jack Oliver who it seems stayed the course with the paper long after most of us had abandoned ship, plus a weekly column from the disc jockey John Peel who was notorious for bringing in his copy in person but usually late. He was a wonderfully witty man, delivering his comments and tales in his own slow dry style which was usually self-deprecating.

He did tell of the night he and a friend (somebody I knew but won't mention) had picked up two girls in a club and gone back to the other chap's flat for an evening of fun and frolics which ended with one young lady throwing up over Peel at a particularly intimate moment. He just said in his Liverpool accent, "I often have that effect on women."

As a sub, the weekly round was much the same as at *MBW* and *MM* - take the copy, read it, edit it, cast it off (still badly in my case), design the page and send it all off to the printers on one of the vans that arrived regularly at the office. They came from Windsor where our printers Oxley were based – and had been for decades.

Our allotted day for printing was Tuesday and that meant I travelled from Paddington to Slough on a main line train and then changed to a quaint pull and push number that took me to Windsor.

Oxley, which was part of the local Windsor newspaper, were set in their ways and I'm not sure they were at all impressed with producing a successful, popular but frivolous (in their eyes) pop music paper, but we got through each week without too many mishaps.

The printers did, however, tell of the day when Rod Stewart, who lived somewhere nearby, was driven down the High Street in a fancy Italian sports car, jumped out and ran round Woolworths before leaping back into his car and zooming off, leaving shop assistants screaming and the good ladies of Windsor somewhat bemused.

Spending my day in Windsor was a delight. I found a splendid American style burger restaurant for lunch and on occasions made my way to Eton College where there was a branch of Coutts (my bank of choice) which was handy for the Queen when she was in town. It was also convenient for the rich kids at Eton and more than once I found myself in a queue behind a diminutive schoolboy in frock coat and top hat as he collected cash from the family account.

There was, however, a rock 'n' roll highlight (and almost a world exclusive) when I got on the train and found myself in a carriage with a long-haired, dishevelled character who was dressed from head to foot in black. I looked – and

looked again – and recognised him as Jimmy Page, star ax-
eman from Led Zeppelin and noted media recluse.

I knew he was a follower of Aleister Crowley, a believer
in the dark arts and what he called "magick." In fact Page
bought the noted occultist's house in Scotland in 1971, and
it has to be said, on this particular day, he looked fairly
scary and very mysterious, even sitting quietly in a British Rail second class compartment. And it was an occasion
when discretion got the better of valour and I gave up on
the idea of a possible world exclusive interview for fear of
upsetting the great man and maybe being turned into a frog
or – some hope - a handsome prince.

Among the most regular visitors to *Disc* were, not surprisingly, the publicists who were trying to earn their fees by
persuading music journalists to interview one of their acts.
Some like Keith Altham, who looked after The Who, Slade,
Marc Bolan and Status Quo, and Tony Brainsby, who represented Paul McCartney, Queen and The Faces, had a head
start because of their star-studded roster. And they were
not above the odd bit of bartering to get some coverage for
a new or lesser known act.

The conversation went along these lines, "Talk to this boy
(or girl) - and believe me they're going to be big – and when
Mick or Paul (insert a star name here) are going to do something I'll take care of you." And who was going to be brave
enough to turn down an offer like that and deny your paper the chance of a major interview with the likes of Jagger
or McCartney? I'm not sure how many of these deals ever
came off as the major acts usually spoke to everyone when
it came to promoting a new album or tour.

Brainsby was a larger than life character who dressed like
a rock star as he went about creating a genuine PR empire.
He hired glamorous assistants such as Caroline Crowther

(daughter of TV star Leslie Crowther) and Magenta Devine who spent every day hidden behind her dark glasses and he was notoriously guilty of giving his pet dog a tab of acid – thankfully it survived.

It was in Brainsby's office when I discovered to my surprise that not all rock stars knew each other. I assumed that, rather like footballers, they all met in clubs, toured together or at least bumped into each other in a motorway cafe. But apparently that wasn't the case as I found out when chatting to Thin Lizzy's Philip (never Phil) Lynott and noticed the incredibly hairy Ian Hunter from Mott The Hoople hanging around. I didn't know him and it was obvious that he had never met Lynott so in the spirit of good rock relations I did the honours and then left them to discuss the merits of something or dish the dirt on somebody.

Other publicists struggled enthusiastically with a collection of acts that hadn't yet made it, might make it somewhere down the line or were never ever going to make it. Among the most persistent were Keith Goodwin and Bill Harry, two ex-journalists turned PRs who sadly didn't have the biggest or best of rosters but boy did they persevere.

In an effort to stop being hassled, a good natured scribe (me included) would agree to a chat (usually a brief one) in the Golden Egg or Red Lion - and you usually ended up buying the drinks. Sadly, the truth was that often nothing ever appeared in the paper and the writer was left to find a way out, usually claiming that the printers or a sub had lost their feature or that a more senior staffer had spiked it because there was no more space in the paper. It was cruel but both publicists and journalists understood the game.

These two venues were both places people from all the various IPC magazines ate regularly, either in the course of work or just for lunch. The Red Lion offered a reasonable bar menu of pies or sandwiches while the Golden Egg, with its egg-shaped menus and gaudy vinyl seats, served chips with most things plus of course eggs prepared in many different ways. Their standard sausage and chips (surprisingly sans eggs) was a bargain at 3s. 9d (17p), the same price as egg, bacon and chips, while their ice cream Alaskan Delight and banana treat Jamaican Longboat both ran to 3s (15p) .

There were also occasional visits to the eaterie in Holborn that had been opened by boxing champion Billy Walker which sold only baked potatoes, with a selection of fancy fillings, and was called, to avoid any confusion, The Baked Potato. This eating house was not Walker's first business venture outside boxing as he and his brother George opened a club cleverly named The Upper Cut in Forest Gate in December 1966. On the opening night gentlemen paid 17s. 6d (87p) and ladies just 15s (75p) to see The Who, while later offerings included The Small Faces and Cream for just 8s 6d (42p).

Further down Fleet Street, at number 148, was probably the best known eating house for both journalists and printers. Mick's Café was open 24 hours a day, offered fry-ups, a variety of meat dishes accompanied by mash or chips and puddings that all went with custard. It was described as "a good old newspaperman's café" and its claim to fame is being the inspiration for the "all night café" referred to in Ralph McTell's famous song 'Streets of London'.

As a sub editor part of the job was dreaming up headlines to go with the features and I think I came up with some winners in my time. A headline can make a feature stand out, make it more memorable or, in some cases, be more entertaining than the story. The best example for me was a *Sun* headline on a story that West Ham player Julian

Dicks was unable to play because of a muscle problem. And what did the keepers of the nation's morals at the country's biggest-selling newspaper come up with … "Swollen Dicks Out." Not classy or subtle but you had to laugh.

I'm not sure where they stand in the pantheon of great headlines but for a feature on Andy Williams I came up with "Handy Andy" while for Bob Harris taking over as host on *The Old Grey Whistle Test* I thought "Bob Faces The Test" was more than good enough. A feature on Irish rock band Thin Lizzy was headed "Dublin Rock" and for my review of Stevie Wonder's album *Talking Book* we ran with "The book according to Stevie." And incidentally I tipped it as the album of 1973 and that was in January!

But even subs are allowed their favourites and I reckon that the headline on my own interview with ELO drummer Bev Bevan ranks up there, although you may have to be of a certain age to get it. "An Hour in Bevan's company" was a play on the name of 1950s Labour politician Aneurin Bevan. My effort for a feature on Elton John's guitarist Davey Johnstone, who described his style of playing as straightforward, even brought a nod of approval (via his publicist) from Elton. It read "The straight man in Elton's camp."

Not so pleased however was Max Bygraves who actually called me to complain about the heading I put on our interview. He objected to "Not at all plastic Max" on the grounds that it was frivolous and didn't do him justice. Another person who might have been upset – if they got the joke – was a reader who was moved to write a letter complaining about my coverage of soul music.

Having passed the letters page over to me to edit and lay out, editor Gavin Petrie was adamant that I include the letter even though it slagged me off. I agreed with the proviso that I could write a snappy, witty sub-headline to go above the letter and that he (Petrie) wouldn't change it. On the provision that it wasn't obscene or libellous, he agreed and the letter appeared in *Disc* under the two words "Ah soul." There was nothing more to say or write and I carried on covering soul music for the paper and never heard another word from my 'fan'.

The headline in *Disc* in early 1973 which upset Max Bygraves who turned out to be a reluctant hit maker with his Singalong series but a natty dresser – thanks to Ted!

MAX BYGRAVES ... NOT INTO THE DISC BUSINESS

Not at all plastic Max

As an entertainer, Max prefers the stage to anything else. TV and films are all very well, but his heart is

Sometimes, but it has to be said not very often, the writers actually got a response from the person they interviewed and Andrew Tyler was the recipient of a telegram from Ringo Starr after their get together which said "8/10 Well done Love Ringo."

An awful lot of interviews we did on *Disc* were carried out on the phone and usually involved a Transatlantic call with me ringing America or an artist calling me at an agreed time. Out in the Essex countryside where I lived we had a fairly unsophisticated phone service which involved having to ask the operator to get the number or the local switchboard girl calling to make sure I was who I was and would accept the call – not the charges!

I spoke to Stevie Wonder, David Gates from Bread, Dr Hook, The Detroit Spinners, New York City and songwriter Ellie Greenwich and most went smoothly although my local operator was overwhelmed to know that she had actually put me through to the real life Stevie Wonder. In fact she called me back at the end of the call to make sure it was him.

On the other hand my call to Billy Paul who was in the offices of Columbia Records, went down a different route. When the international operator got through to the Columbia switchboard and asked for Mr Paul, she was told that there was nobody of that name in the company. She asked "What does he do?" and I then piped up to say that he was currently topping the US chart with 'Me And Mrs Jones' and was probably her company's top selling artist at the moment. Then they found him.

Music papers have been rock 'n' roll and maybe a bit raunchy – certainly a lot of the adverts for albums back then featured scantily clad women – but there was still a strict code when it came to certain words. We might have run with a 'bloody' or even a "shit" – and that wasn't a certainty – but words beginning with 'f' or 'c' were definitely verboten so we never contemplated explaining what the American band called SNAFU actually stood for. In fact nobody in the office knew and it was some years before an American explained to me that it was a military phrase – popular in the Vietnam War – which stood for "Situation Normal All F***** Up"

And on that note there was never any chance that I was going to include all the stuff I was told in my phone call with Dr Hook, who were residing somewhere in the Deep South. It began with me being told that Ray Sawyer (the one with the eye patch) is Dr Hook but that I would be talking to Dennis Locorriere who, it was explained, "Isn't Dr Hook but is the leader." The whole conversation took a turn for the unsavoury early on with Locorriere telling me how he was arrested for obscenity, that the band had posed naked except for discreetly placed socks for a magazine and finally explaining the meaning of the phrase "sloppy seconds" which is not something I am going to repeat in this family-friendly tome.

Nudity reared its ugly head again when I went round to interview the singer Andy Williams, the clean-cut crooner whose fans included my mum. When photographer Mike Putland and I arrived at the house he was renting close to Hyde Park, we were let in by his PR lady and climbed a mountain of stairs to find the great man out on his small balcony, lying on a lounger – and stark naked. I whispered to Putland to get a few snaps of him in the all-together but he was too much of a professional to stoop that low (Williams was flat out). Eventually Williams covered himself with a kimono and then surprised me some more by outlining a few of his great loves in life … The Rolling Stones,

Photographer Mike Putland didn't snap singer Andy Williams reclining nude on a sun lounger in his London retreat but waited until the American star decided to cover up in a kimono for the interview and photo session. (Photograph by Mike Putland)

John Lennon's album *Imagine* and "seeing kids enjoying an open air concert in the sun with a bottle of wine and smoking grass." He was now a star in my eyes.

Most of the face to face interviews we did took place in a bar, café or the offices of the record company, manager or publicist, but there were occasions when you were actually invited to a star's home. My first house call was to Elton John's opulent place in the very upmarket area of Virginia Water and it was suitably crammed with a pinball machine, a suit of armour and some stuffed animals, although it was the warthog in reception that took my eye. It was a memorable introduction to the way stars live and his mum was on hand to bring in the tea and biccies.

My next visit was to see and interview the man who led the Who. But Pete Townshend's imposing Thameside home in Twickenham was not easy to find. I was helped out by a street cleaner pushing a dustcart who told me, "That's it, some pop geezer lives there." In fact the "pop geezer" lived in a rambling weather-boarded mansion which had, parked out front, a huge American coach, a fancy Mercedes (complete with smoked windows) and an ugly American Dodge saloon with huge rocket fins.

Inside, while children trundled across the dining area on scooters, we sought refuge on the stairs where there was a small statue of Meher Baba, an Indian spiritual master who claimed to be a "God in human form." He had died in 1969 and Townshend was a follower of his teachings and had dedicated the album we were there to talk about to Baba's memory.

Although it was always unlikely that I, or any other journalist, would ever be invited to the home (or should that be homes) of Diana Ross, I was allowed to meet her in one of London's poshest hotels when she came to London for the opening of her film *Lady Sings The Blues*. She held court in a small suite and took us writers on six at a time with the next six waiting on the side lines like substitutes at a football match. It was all pretty haphazard as we fired questions in the allotted 20-minute session and tried to note down her answers while a posse of helpers saw to the great lady's every need. "Can we get a drink for Miss Ross?", "Where are the tissues for Miss Ross?" or "Do you have some stirrers for Miss Ross' drink?" Did I forget to mention that we all had to call her 'Miss Ross' too?

Twenty plus years ahead of the TV series *Through The Keyhole*,

I got to poke around and share some time with Elton John

in his Virginia Water home complete with a suit of armour

and stuffed animals ... while his mum served us tea

Another hotel interview, this time in the Savoy, was with one of my songwriting heroes Randy Newman, who had an impressive suite overlooking the River Thames; not bad for a man who the previous evening had played to a just about half full Royal Festival Hall. It was his first concert in the UK and he thought it went OK, telling me "It was all I could have expected". Lounging ("I like lying down, I'm pretty good at it"), he explained - in t-shirt, jeans and bare feet - that plans for him to appear in a movie about Beethoven had been a hoax. "That was a joke a couple of us thought up and sent to the papers. Me as Beethoven in a movie called *I Can't Hear.*"

In the early 1970s, and before *Disc* was the byword for music industry awards, the magazine introduced its own rewards scheme in 1959 and presented silver discs for records that sold over 250,000 and gold for anything that passed the one million mark. These prizes were handed out on the back of sales figures supplied by record companies and I'm not sure what sort of checking went on to authenticate the numbers, but in 1973 the British Phonographic Industry (BPI) took over and began the industry's official awards scheme that still runs to this day.

Disc was also home to its own Valentine's Awards, voted for by readers, and handed out each year at a (hopefully) star-studded event in London's West End. The name Valentine had nothing to do with Penny Valentine, the magazine's most famous writer, but was adopted once it was decided to award the prizes around February 14 each year. I only got to one of these – the 1973 event which was held in a swanky London disco where, if I remember rightly, Marc Bolan stole the show while an up and coming singer called Shakin' Stevens with his band the Sunsets turned in a vintage rock 'n' roll performance.

A music writer's life could be tough and this time it involved taking
tea and making notes in a suite at the Savoy Hotel with singer songwriter Randy Newman (left).But when it came to picking a photo
to go with my feature, *Disc* went with one of just Newman and
cut me out. (Photograph by Mike Putland)

As the third best-selling music paper in the UK, *Disc* did
not get offered too many trips overseas to review shows or
interview bands on the road.

Any 'freebies' to America were, it seemed, exclusively
handed out to *MM* and *New Musical Express* which was also
part of the IPC empire but located on the other side of the
River Thames in Southwark.

But if the US was off limits, there were trips to Europe
and mine included going to Hamburg to see and talk to the
US all-girl group Fanny where guitarist June Millington
told me that she kept a diary of all things Fanny-related,
although it was never going to be published.

"It's too sordid," she said which is probably just as well as
her bandmate Alice de Buhr confided to me that the only

problem she had with being on the road was, "When I get horny."

Germany again, and this time it was to Frankfurt for a double whammy to interview and review both Al Green and Gilbert O'Sullivan on successive nights in the same city. The trip to Frankfurt was courtesy of Decca who had both acts and astutely saw the chance to make the best of a good opportunity and offer me a 'twofer' deal.

Green, a soul hero of mine, was both brilliant and charming while O'Sullivan was a surprising revelation – funny and far more outgoing than I expected.

Backstage in Frankfurt Germany with soul singer Al Green (left) and by now we were into the latest technology as notepad and pen were replaced by a fancy tape recorder and microphone

However the abiding memory of the trip is O'Sullivan's musical director and orchestra leader Johnnie Spence (he did the same job for Tom Jones and Engelbert Humperdinck) telling stories about Elvis Presley, who it seemed was a strange cove with a liking for what he called "real velvet", and his own time as a raw recruit in the British Army.

Unable to manage the obligatory left, right, left, right marching sequence, he was pulled up by his sergeant major who poked his swagger stick into Spence's chest and said "Do you know what's on the end of this stick Spence?" The London born musician replied "No sir." Then, when the officer told him "It's a c***, Spence," the band leader replied "Not on this end Sarge." Spence, who died the day before Presley in 1977, said he spent the next two weeks in an army prison cell.

Chapter 21

WHEN THE EARTH (AND WOLVERHAMPTON) MOVED

There were also two trips to Dublin to see Thin Lizzy play in their hometown. Trip number one saw me travel solo to a gig in February and it coincided with the band becoming the first home-grown act to actually top the singles chart in Ireland with 'Whisky In The Jar', ahead of Them and Rory Gallagher ... and U2.

I am delighted to say that after this trip the band's leader Philip Lynott became a friend, visiting my home and my office at EMI – usually for a free lunch and some free albums. He was a softly spoken giant of a man with all the charm and wit that went with being Irish and on my trip to his home city, after a couple of hot chocolates and breakfast butties, he took me on a tour of the highlights of Dublin. The tour ended in a pub near the centre where, he said, we would find the folk band the Dubliners. And sure enough some of them were looking slightly worse for the drink and a little bit ferocious.

In between visiting Ireland, in March 1973, the relative peace of a Wednesday afternoon in the *Disc* office was shattered by a loud explosion when an IRA car bomb went off outside the Old Bailey. One person died and nearly 250 people were injured and, despite us being a good quarter of a mile away, the blast rattled the windows and those of us on chairs with castors suddenly took an unscheduled trip across the room.

A month later I went back to Dublin with my wife for Thin Lizzy's concert at the National Stadium and we stayed in some luxury at the famous Gresham Hotel in the city's O'Connell Street. It had been the setting for part of the James Joyce story *The Dead* and it was from there that we set out, with the band's publicist Brainsby at the wheel, for the venue. Hopelessly lost, we stopped at a set of traffic lights and asked a man on a bicycle if he knew the way to the National Stadium. He looked at us, said "Yes" and cycled off.

Even without help from a 'local' we found the venue and enjoyed a riotous evening but It was the next day when things got more interesting as flights to London were being delayed or cancelled. Pat and I and the band's manager Chris Morrison were in danger of being marooned in Dublin. Sensing our predicament, a helpful member of the band's crew said he knew a man who could fly us into the UK but we would be dropped off in a field somewhere near Liverpool.

I wasn't sure if he was serious but we declined his kind offer, preferring to deal with Aer Lingus who finally put us on standby for the next flight, or the one after that or the one after that - nobody really knew and after a while nobody really cared.

But the fun really started as we went through Customs to

the departure lounge. I declared half a dozen cans of genuine Irish Guinness (for my dad you understand) while Morrison showed the officers a case full of money and some paperwork.

He was carrying the band's share of the takings from their Irish shows which he had changed into English pounds at a local bank where he had been given whatever documents you needed to cart around a few thousand quid in a briefcase. We took our seats in the lounge and all was well until a couple of plain clothes Special Branch men arrived to talk to Morrison about his bag of lolly.

He explained that he was the manager of Thin Lizzy, explained where the money had come from and showed them the paperwork.

Then events took an unexpected turn as one of the officers admitted that his daughter was a huge fan of the band and asked if we had any merchandise. Morrison passed over some stickers and posters and then pulled the surprise rabbit out of the hat by telling them that I, with my long hair and fancy gear, was in fact the band's drummer Brian Downey.

Despite being three years older, an inch shorter and born in the Midlands I was a dead ringer for him – after all we had the same first name – and I managed to get out of saying anything in a dodgy Irish accent but happily signed the posters and all was well with the world as we travelled back to London.

This skulduggery involving signing star's autographs was something that I would repeat during my time on tour with the Carpenters when I signed glossy 10x8 photographs of the duo. For two weeks in 1974, I practiced and perfected my Karen Carpenter signature on pictures which were handed out to fans at the stage door, in hotels or at airports.

The launch party for Thin Lizzy's Vagabonds Of The Western World album in September 1973 but who is that in the back row between band members Philip Lynott (2nd left) and Eric Bell? Could it be drummer Brian Downey or author Brian Southall who was introduced as him to security at Dublin Airport by manager Chris Morrison (next to Bell). Actually it's Southall trying to look the part as Downey was missing from the launch

I had done interviews in houses, hotels, offices and cramped backstage areas but going to see Max Bygraves in his dressing room before his afternoon matinee show at the New Victoria Theatre was a brand new experience.

I had argued with the editor that we should somehow feature Bygraves in the paper as he was a hit act with his *Singalong With Max* albums - Volumes 1 & 2 – high in the charts (and two more would follow). So off I went to see the man who, years earlier, had given us classics such as 'Cowpuncher's Cantata' and 'Gilly Gilly Ossenfeffer Katzenellen Bogen By The Sea'. He was, by his own admission, an unlikely chart entry, explaining "I'm really an entertainer. I'm not in the disc business" but as a top of the bill act and a star for over 20 years, there were perks that went with the job and Ted was one of them.

Ted was Bygraves' dresser and as he scurried about doing his business, I sat with pen poised and notebook in hand and interviewed Bygraves who was undressed and then re-dressed in his stage outfit and brought make-up which he applied himself. It was a surreal moment talking to Max Bygraves as trousers were removed and replaced but I got over it even though the man himself was moved to call and complain about the headline.

Every now and again we did features that were not based around interviews with artists but were in-depth pieces where we investigated and reported back on issues such as which pop acts were classically trained musicians, whether The Osmonds were better than The Beatles and the relevance of Elvis Presley in 1972.

I did all three of these articles and explained that Slade's Jimmy Lea, singer/songwriter Peter Skellern and three members of ELO – violinist Wilf Gibson, cellists Colin Walker and Mike Edwards – were all classically trained, and I then astutely decided that The Osmonds were just "pretty faces" while The Beatles were an "exception to every rule in pop music."

The feature on Elvis came out in January 1973 just after his 38th birthday – I noted that he shared his birthday with my mum (January 8) but they never sent cards to each other – and confirmed that he had had a very good year despite

being written off by some critics. Looking back it was perhaps unfortunate that I wrote that the King is "nowhere
near dead or buried" beneath a headline that said he was
"the legend that refuses to die." How was I supposed to
know that he would be dead within four years at the age of
just 42, but at least lauded as the first artist to sell over one
billion records.

One of the hardest tasks I was given in 1973 was to write
the life story of Suzi Quatro in four parts – with each article
displayed as a centre spread over one month. Weirdly the
lady in question had had, by my calculations, only two hits
by the end of that summer ('Can The Can' and '48 Crash')
so it may have been a trifle early to detail the life of a mere
23-year-old. But that was my task and I have to admit it
was tough trying to pad out feature after feature and a long
lunch time session in a fancy Mayfair pub didn't make it
any easier … and not being a fan made it doubly hard. I
asked 'why me?' back then and still ask it to this day.

Years later I occasionally ran into Ms Quatro at Chelmsford railway station as she travelled to London from her
home in the nearby village of Little Walthm but as she
never raised the subject of my 'life-story', I saw no reason
to mention it either.

Getting free records to review (or just keep) was a definite
bonus for all us music journos but there was another sort
of secret perk that went with the job. Any albums that you
didn't want could be sold and our favourite go-to dealer
was Asman's in Covent Garden.

It was a specialist jazz shop but they were not above taking all our spares and presumably selling them on. About
once a month we would get a taxi from Fleet Street armed
with boxes of albums as we also served as the go-betweens
for more famous Radio 1 disc jockeys and producers who

had buckets of albums to get rid of. These stars of the air-waves were anxious not to be seen toting armfuls of albums around town, so we less recognisable scribes acted as the middle men for people who we presumed might have been fired from the Beeb had they been caught collecting extra cash. Their case woul;d not have been helped by the fact that the records we sold came from the record companies with a sticker saying 'promotional copy – not for resale' which we (and Mr Asman) chose to ignore.

Life as a music journalist had many more up-sides – see-ing top bands in concert, reviewing quality albums (and both for free) and then actually meeting those artists who fell into the category of 'heroes.' For me Harry Nilsson was up there among the greats and in the spring of 1973 I some-how got invited to meet and interview the American who had charted with 'Everybody's Talkin' in 1969 and hit num-ber one with 'Without You' in 1972.

He was an enigma, a man who gave very few interviews and never performed live but was lauded by both John Lennon and Paul McCartney who named him as their "fa-vourite singer and group"(?) in the late sixties. For reasons that to this day I don't understand, our almost resident pho-tographer Mike Putland asked me if I would be interested in being involved in the design of the cover for Nilsson's 1972 album *Son of Schmilsson* which required some fancy 'vampire lettering' to resemble dripping blood. I think (and hope) that he put my name forward but unfortunately nothing more came of it, although Putland did get to pho-tograph the cover.

Having missed out on one chance to perhaps meet Nils-son and swap design ideas, I got a call from somebody at his record company asking if I wanted to go to the studios in Wembley and interview the singer as he recorded his album *A Little Touch of Schmilsson in the Night*. I think my excited response was probably along the lines of 'would I … try and stop me?'

Nilsson was there with his producer Derek Taylor, the former press officer for the Beatles and Apple who I had met on a couple of occasions, and engineer Phil McDonald who had worked on a host of Beatles tracks between 1966 and 1970. We assembled in a small room inside CTS Studios in Wembley, close to the home of football, where Nilsson held forth on the album, which was being arranged by Gordon Jenkins (best known for his work with Frank Sinatra), his choice of classic songs dating back to the 1920s, the ability of Ringo Starr as a drummer and the problems with performing live concerts.

"I've had the idea for a couple of years but never had the balls to do it," explained Nilsson when talking about the album. "Everyone loves these songs and it's the best and easiest damn session I've ever done." As for The Beatles' drummer, the singer simply said, "He's the best there is", while Nilsson's reason for not performing live was slightly more complex.

He said that the thought of going out on stage to find an empty auditorium would be awful and embarrassing. When I told him that would never be the case as his fans would flock in their thousands to see and hear him, he looked aghast and replied, "That would be even worse, having all those people out there." That was his argument and it was hard not to see where he was coming from although I found out later that he had been known to perform in the early hours at a piano in the bar of a London hotel near his Mayfair flat, which was where both Mama Cass and Keith Moon died while staying there – without Nilsson.

Having spent an afternoon with Nilsson, Taylor then

asked if I wanted to go along to the next day's recording and filming of a TV special for BBC 2 featuring the singer, Jenkins and a full orchestra at the Beeb's Shepherd's Bush Theatre in London. Knowing full well that I was never going to get another chance to see Nilsson perform, I said yes and even blagged an invitation for my wife to come along.

The theatre, home to many popular BBC shows such as *Crackerjack, Juke Box Jury* and *The Generation Game*, was full of musicians and the Taylor family – Derek's wife and their many children – plus a few necessary TV and record company people but, and this was important, no other journalists. This was my exclusive moment

The only disappointment was that the session we sat through was miked to focus on the orchestra and not Nilsson's vocals which were being recorded during another session but he was there and he sang along, to help with intros and timings, so we got just a taste of *Harry Nilsson In Concert* ... and it was a joyous and unforgettable experience.

But life wasn't all about features and interviews, there were always concerts to be reviewed and you did your best to be fair and tried to avoid going along to shows by acts that you really didn't like – that would have been unfair on everyone. However, I did review Tom Jones at the London Palladium but only so I could take my mum who brought along sandwiches and cakes for my tea. Despite my mum enjoying every moment, I suggested that it "wasn't a particularly good show" and that the Jones boy "lacked all the glamour and sexuality I imagined he'd generate." This was something that his manager Gordon Mills, who was known to be highly protective of his stable of artists, took issue with when he and I met at some other event but we worked things out amicably.

I was kinder to American Billy Preston when he played the Rainbow Theatre, saying that after a slow start he "shone through as a real professional and a very, very good keyboards man," while I reckoned The Temptations at Hammersmith Odeon came across as "as good a vocal group as any around ... slick, talented and professional."

Then there was the joy and delight in seeing one of my newest fave bands (and they were now my first rock 'n' roll friends), Thin Lizzy, at Birmingham Town Hall in late 1973. It would turn out to be one of the last shows I reviewed for *Disc* and having seen the band a few times I was well qualified to suggest that they were "improving with every gig" and were "stronger than they have ever been."

One show I went to with Pat but didn't review involved a trip to Wolverhampton to see Slade's return home gig at the Civic Hall in June 1973 when the 3000-seater auditorium, built in 1938, was given a hammering by fans of the local quartet. We went along with Mike Ledgerwood and his girlfriend and, as the most local, I was in charge of translating and giving directions to our 'black country' taxi driver while the other three sat in the back, baffled by the man's accent.

It was an extraordinary night, the first time I had ever seen a balcony actually move up and down as fans screamed and leapt about as their heroes ploughed through their list of hit singles – eight up to that time including five number ones. After the show we all trooped back to the band's favourite pub, The Trumpet in Bilston, which had on display the licensee's impressive collection of records ... all stuck to the ceiling.

Two things stand out from that night when I first met former Animals bass player Chas Chandler who had managed Jimi Hendrix and now managed Slade. It was the first

time I had visited a gents toilet to find people snorting co-
caine; I knew it went on but not in my house so to speak,
so it came as a shock when the culprits (no names) huddled
together to keep prying eyes off their gear. The second
revelation came in a conversation with guitarist Dave Hill
who, and he may have been joking, said that the first thing
he was going to do with his new found wealth was "buy a
big house overlooking a girls' school's playing field." There
is no acceptable answer to that sort of ambition but all I can
say is that it was the seventies and not whatever the 'woke'
2020s are called.

*****

While *MM*'s small adverts were famous for bringing musicians together - and *NME* did their bit with an ad that
linked Bernie Taupin with Elton John – *Disc* was never in
the position of being a recruiting agency for lost musical
souls in search of an outlet for their talents. We did no more
than feature a 'Bargain Basement' page of classifieds offering readers a chance to buy the latest in Loon Pants (£2.85p
a pair with a 28" flare), stars and stripes singlets (£1.20p),
US army cloth badges (four for 95p) and Balakrishna joss
sticks (12 packets for 85p). It was a veritable treasure trove
of goodies for the hippest teenagers around.

When I joined the paper Mike Ledgerwood was probably *Disc*'s longest serving staff member and during over
a decade in the music business he had assembled a list of
contacts in a black book – both business and social (ladies)
– which he guarded like a Russian spy's code book. As news
editor, he was charged with finding out what was going on
in the 'biz', unearthing the truth from the gossip and wild
rumours and delivering it all in time for us on the subs desk

to create the two or three news pages at the front of the paper.

The front page story was always the biggest news of the week and if we didn't have a genuine major story about a band splitting or re-forming or touring or releasing a new album, there were always our fallback options such as "Elvis to tour UK?" or "Beatles to re-form?" And the question mark was always the giveaway because we knew deep down that neither of these things were ever going to happen, but you could always get a quote from somebody (anybody in Ledgerwood's black book) to give us enough copy for a few paragraphs to go with a big photo.

Being both a fan and a fellow Midlander (although not quite a Brummie) I formed some sort of allegiance with Roy Wood and all the things that came from the ex-Move man, which included creating ELO, leaving to assemble Wizzard and making a solo album ... all within two years. I interviewed Rick Price when he joined Wizzard, spoke with Bev Bevan on life in ELO and did at least three features with Wood himself when he created Wizzard, recorded his solo album *Boulders* and reflected on his life in music. And there was a double-hander with my colleague Caroline Boucher when she wrote about Jeff Lynne and ELO and I covered Roy and Wizzard in a piece headlined "Both Sides Now."

As is often the case in life there was a quid pro quo in all these dealings and I soon found myself interviewing Ayshea Brough, the one-time daughter-in-law of radio ventriloquist (yes, there were such things) Peter Brough and host of a popular children's TV show called *Lift Off* which according to her "made me a star in many ways." More relevant was the fact that she was also the lady in Roy Wood's life back in the summer of 1973 and, surprise, surprise, he was also the writer and producer of her new single. Although this release failed to trouble the chart compilers it didn't stop her, for reasons I never found out, going on to represent Spain in a song contest held in what we knew then as Yugoslavia.

Whatever the price, I enjoyed Wood's company in addition to his music, even if he did get me into trouble with one of rock's legendary danger men. It wasn't often that I got to write a front page lead headline story – that was Ledgerwood's domain – but just once I came up with the goods and, again, it involved Wood. Over a meal one evening he told me about his plans for his new rock 'n' roll band Wizzard to play at Wembley Stadium alongside Bill Haley, Chuck Berry and Billy Fury at the so-called "London Rock 'n' Roll Festival."

This was big news and I had got it exclusively from the horse's mouth so to speak and I served it up to Ledgerwood as a page one scoop. The downside was that Wood's manager, the notorious Don Arden, who was nicknamed the 'Yiddish Godfather of Rock' and had a reputation for what were called "aggressive business tactics", wasn't ready for the news to be released to the press.

I had jumped the gun and this meant a phone call from Arden demanding to know where I had got the news, while at the same time denying it was true. When I nervously blurted out that Roy had told me the other evening and never mentioned that it was a secret, Arden shouted, "Alright then but next time be careful." I had no idea what he meant - was it a threat, was I to be banned from all future events involving Roy Wood or just be careful crossing the road?

There were odd visitors to the offices of *Disc* as publicists would often take an artist on a hopeful stroll along the corridor on the off chance of generating some interest with somebody on either *MM* and *Disc* (or even *MBW* on a bad day). There were also rumours that both Bob Dylan and Paul Simon had visited the offices in Fleet Street in the sixties in an attempt to further their careers, but I could never find anybody who had actually been there or seen them.

At *Disc* I recall Arthur Brown – he of the "Crazy World of" and the hit single 'Fire' – coming in to see Boucher while ex-Bee Gees drummer Colin Petersen was a friend of Ledgerwood and called in regularly.

Then there was David Essex, brought in by his dedicated manager Derek Bowman who was adamant that his 23-year-old singer, who had landed the lead part in the musical *Godspell*, was all set for stardom … and at the end of the day he was right.

It was not unusual for a music journalist to strike up a sort of friendship with a musician although they rarely lasted longer than the need for a bit of publicity. For some reason I became acquainted with Rod Linton who was a guitarist on John Lennon's wonderful *Imagine* album and, on the back of doing a small feature on his time in the studio with the former Beatle, we lunched and drank together a few times before we all moved on. Another odd 'friendship;' was with American Bruce Johnston who had been fired from The Beach Boys in early 1972. I presume I talked to him about his plans to record a solo album – I can't remember anything about it or even what it was called – but somehow he decided that I was his new best English buddy.

This involved him calling me at home (when a Beach Boy – even an ex-one - asks you for your home telephone number you give it up) in the middle of my night but during his day for no particular reason other than to chat aimlessly and endlessly. Despite my explanations about the time difference, which he said he understood, this went on for a while before he presumably got bored, saw the size of his phone bill or found a new pal.

He did, during a call to the office late in my afternoon, tell me a story about him being in a bed with a lady friend in Los Angeles when a minor earthquake struck the city and she, according to Johnston, uttered the immortal words, "It felt like the earth moved." It was a great line but there was part of me that thought he probably wasn't the first bloke in California to claim that line for a post-coital finale.

*****

Things were changing at *Disc* as David Hughes left to become head of press at Polydor Records and soon after Mike Ledgerwood took on the same role with A&M Records. And things would change for me too but not before I had done an interview with a relatively unknown singer-songwriter who would crop up again and again in my life.

The publicist Bill Harry had called me, probably from the Red Lion, to say he was "downstairs" with an artist who was going to be a huge star and that he was someone I had worked with. I was intrigued, so I said OK and went down to meet this person from my past and it turned out to be Steve Harley who had joined the *Braintree & Witham Times* (as Steve Nice) just after I left. So, we hadn't exactly worked together but it was close enough for Harry.

Harley and I chatted and we reminisced about people we both knew from the papers in Braintree and in nearby Colchester before moving on to his new career as leader of Cockney Rebel. In the autumn of 1973 they had not had any hit records, were on the cusp of releasing their debut album but, echoing the words of his publicist, Harley did tell me what the future held for him; "I am going to be a star.

A star with a capital S" And you read it first in *Disc* from the pen of Brian Southall – also with a capital S

Harley did go on to become a star, probably no thanks to my article, and in my later life at EMI our paths crossed again as he released a host of hit records for the company. There was a falling-out when we dropped him but things were patched up years later when we both attended a retirement party for an ex-colleague from our days on the local papers in Essex and since then there has been a constant round of lunches and dinners out in the wilds of East Anglia.

Very soon after talking to Steve Harley in a Fleet Street hostelry I packed away my pen and notebook and gave up being a journalist to join Ledgerwood in the press office at A&M. I became another in a long line of poachers who turned gamekeeper – a role I would continue to play for the next thirty years.

And make of this what you will – and apportion credit or blame as you see fit – but the three local papers I worked on in the 1960s are all still in business while the 'glam' titles of *Music Business Weekly*, *Goal*, *Melody Maker* and *Disc* have all gone out of business. And of the three record companies I worked for, two (A&M and EMI) were snapped up by the French-owned Universal Music while one other (Warner Music) was bought by a Ukranian billionaire.

To slightly mis-quote the great Nobel prize winner Bob Dylan, "the times have certainly been a-changing."

Over 50 years on and here I am with a copy of
Music Business Weekly from 1969, the year I
moved to Fleet Street, joined IPC's Longacre
Press and began a near forty year career in
the music business.
(Photo: David Roberts)

Biblography

Readers of *A Saucerful of Tea* may be interested to check out this list of Brian Southall's other books:

Abbey Road (Patrick Stephens 1982/ Omnibus 1997)
A-Z of Record Labels (Sanctuary Books 2000)
Northern Songs (Omnibus 2006)
Sex Pistols - 90 Days at EMI (Bobcat 2007)
If You Don't Know Me By Now - Story of Simply Red
(Carlton 2007)
Pop Goes To Court (Omnibus 2008)
The Rise & Fall Of EMI (Omnibus 2009)
Beatles Memorabilia - The Julian Lennon Collection
(Goodman 2010)
Treasures Of The Bee Gees (Carlton 2011)
Jimi Hendrix Made In England (Clarksdale 2012)
Treasures Of Bob Dylan (Carlton 2012)
Dark Side Of the Moon Revealed (Clarksdale 2013)
The Beatles In 100 Objects (Carlton 2013)
From Me To You (Red Planet 2014)
Banned on the Run - The music they wouldn't let you buy
(Poppublishing 2014)
The Hollies Story (Red Planet/Poppublishing 2015)
Sgt. Pepper's Lonely Hearts Club Band (Carlton 2017)
Dreamboats & Petticoats (Red Planet 2017)
The White Album (Carlton 2018)
The Beatles Album By Album (Carlton 2019)
Bringing On Back The Good Times (This Day
In Music Books 2021)

Printed in Great Britain
by Amazon